To:

....

From:

....

FIND HOPE

A devotional journey to trust in God's unfailing love

Best-Selling Author of *For Women Only*

SHAUNTI FELDHAHN

Christian Art Gifts®

Visit Christian Art Gifts, Inc. at www.christianartgifts.com.

Find Hope

Published by Christian Art Gifts Inc., IL, USA

ISBN 978-1-63952-319-1 GB259
ISBN 978-1-63952-405-1 GB253

Printed in China

28 27 26 25 24 23
10 9 8 7 6 5 4 3 2 1

A Personal Note

I'm so grateful you are holding this devotional! Maybe you picked it up, or maybe someone handed it to you. Either way, thanks for joining me on this journey. It is so important, because hope is God's fuel for our lives.

Each of us struggle with all sorts of issues—things like school, relationships, health, job, kids—but as long as we feel hope for the future, we are motivated, right? We can keep going! It is when hope fades that we find it easier to check out, step back, or give up. But a true sense of hope gives us *life.*

Realizing what true hope is.

The trouble is, we often experience what I call "excruciating hope" instead. We say, with a bit of desperation, "I hope my kids stop being rebellious" or "I hope my grades improve," but what we actually mean is, "I worry they won't."

That is hope with a little "h." It has no certainty. And hope with no certainty is just a wish.

There's nothing *wrong* with wishing something would happen, but it cannot fill us with life. We might be pumped up for a time, but then our engine runs down from lack of fuel. We get discouraged or downcast. We may even despair.

In other words, we have no sure strength right when we need it most. Because little-h hope is entirely dependent on specific outcomes.

For example, imagine that you are in a dark season in marriage and aren't optimistic that things can improve. Now imagine that your spouse says, "I love you and I want to make this work." You suddenly feel a sense of hope. But it's solely because there is concrete evidence that circumstances are working out the way you long for them to. Now, of course, good outcomes *should* lead to gratitude for a loving heavenly Father who rescues those in distress and who wants good things for His children.

God wants us to have hope even in—*especially in*—the dark places. This is a Hope with a capital "H"—a supernatural Hope and motivation for the future that has nothing to do with specific outcomes.

How do we find such Hope?

The apostle Paul provides the answer: "I pray that God, the source of hope, will fill you completely with joy and peace *because you trust in him. Then* you will overflow with confident hope through the power of the Holy Spirit" (Romans 15:13 NLT, emphasis added).

In hard times, God leans in, pulls us close, and reminds us that He, not our circumstances, is our source of true hope. He wants us to be saturated with joy and peace not because of what is going on in our lives, but because we trust Him.

The Greek word for "trust" in Romans 15:13, *pisteuō,* implies the *choice* to trust; it is the same word used in the famous John 3:16 explanation, "For God so loved the world that he gave his one and only Son, that whoever believes (*pisteuō*) in him shall not perish but have eternal life." Paul says that as we intentionally give God our trust, His Holy Spirit will flood us with so much confident hope that not only are we fully fueled, but we "overflow"! We will have enough hope to help others keep going as well.

That is the sort of hope we all want; a hope that doesn't sputter when times get hard.

Our process.

In this devotional, we will walk together through ten elements of finding that sort of hope—habits we consistently see in Scripture and even in science.

Our first ten days will introduce each of those habits. Then after that, each day we will go a bit deeper into a specific truth about one of them and briefly reflect on how to apply it to our individual life. By Day 60, we aim to be in a very different place from where we started!

Now, to be clear, we may still need other help along the way. Someone dealing with clinical depression might also need medical treatment. Someone dealing with a marriage or parenting crisis might need to seek counseling. But the beautiful truth is that God has given us ways to go beyond *finding* Hope and actually *build* our Hope and trust in Him!

Are you ready to build this unshakable Hope together? Let's get started.

Shaunti Feldhahn

Elements of Finding Hope

- Keep an Eternal Perspective
- Know Jesus
- Lift Your Eyes
- Live in Humility
- Cast Out Fear
- Trust His Purposes
- Be Salt and Light
- Do the Work
- Redeem Suffering
- Devote Yourself to the Family of God

Day 1

So we don't look at the troubles we can see now;
rather, we fix our gaze on things that cannot be seen.
For the things we see now will soon be gone,
but the things we cannot see will last forever.

—2 Corinthians 4:18, NLT

Live in Light of Eternity

Growing up, the concept of heaven was vague to me. I viewed heaven like I viewed some special foreign city—a beige, soft-focus place I couldn't really picture, but was hoping to get to someday.

Have you ever thought that way? Living our busy lives, we may know eternity exists, but we just can't picture it. And it just doesn't seem *relevant* to our day-to-day experience.

Everything changed when I read Randy Alcorn's novel *Deadline*. I instantly loved a main character and (sorry for the spoiler) was disappointed when he was killed in the very first chapter. But wait! The story showed him crossing into eternity. And from then on, the book took place both on earth and in heaven. He was still a main character . . . he had simply moved to a new place.

As I read, I suddenly had a vision of heaven—based on speculation, of course, but also on biblical principles. For example, various characters prayed in heaven. (As the story pointed out, why would we stop praying when we are even closer to God?) And I saw how many things we care about just don't matter from an eternal perspective.

Meanwhile, other things—such as how we handle suffering and how we interact with others—matter more than we can fathom. It began to drastically change my attitude about daily stressors like financial issues or fighting traffic. What matters more in light of eternity, the fact that I'm going to be an embarrassing fifteen minutes late to a big meeting, or how I conduct myself in the midst of it?

The implications of eternity change everything.

Friends, as you read this, eternity isn't "out there" in some beige future. It is a present reality that has *vast* implications for our day-to-day lives here and now. It is just beyond our sight but even more real and tangible than everything we *do* see here.

If we have given our lives to Christ, we are no longer citizens of this "shadowland" (Matthew 4:16) but of His everlasting Kingdom. Every single day, He has tangible purposes for us here that have an impact for eternity. The question is: are we *living,* every day, like eternity is real? Being able to answer that question with a resounding "yes" is one crucial purpose of this devotional. Because as we do, our hope is no longer vague but becomes solid as rock.

Reflection

How does it make you feel to know that God has a tangible purpose for you today that will have an impact for eternity? Consider a challenge you are facing this week. What might you do differently if you handle it with an eternal perspective in mind?

"Right now counts forever."

—R. C. Sproul

Day 2

But when the Father sends the Advocate as my representative—that is, the Holy Spirit—he will teach you everything and will remind you of everything I have told you.

—John 14:26, NLT

Walking the Hills with Jesus

Have you ever wished that you had been born 2,000 years ago, in order to actually walk the hills with Jesus? To listen to Him in person? Many of us are wistful that we don't have that today. We want to know Jesus more, but often feel distant. And when we face something hard—for example, having been deeply hurt by someone we care about or wrestling with bad news—we can feel rudderless. Even hopeless. We think, *I wish I could walk with Jesus and get His perspective and guidance directly.*

Friends, we still can!

Jesus said that once He left, God the Father would send the Holy Spirit to those who accept Him —not to walk beside us but to be far closer, to actually live *in* us! Jesus' disciples didn't even have that. They could only hear Him when He was physically present. By contrast, God has given us a priceless gift: a two-way street of 24–7 fellowship with Him.

No matter where we are, God's Spirit can teach us all things and bring to our minds everything Jesus told us. And when we open the Bible, it is living and active. So as we pray about how to handle being hurt, and the convicting thought comes to mind, *Maybe I should stop holding a grudge and forgive this person,* that could indeed be God speaking to us—even though we will never hear Him perfectly. Or when we read a Scripture and get that, "Huh, that's interesting" feeling at a particular verse, that's probably the Holy Spirit's prompting.

Let's never ignore or turn down the equivalent of walking the hills with Jesus 24–7! When those prompts come, let's not push past them and go about our day or keep reading in order to finish the chapter. Hope will be birthed as we listen, as we journal what we think we are hearing, and as we ask the Holy Spirit to guide us—in much the same way it would have if we had walked and talked with Jesus 2,000 years ago.

As in any relationship, we must cultivate the back-and-forth. Let's be like the psalmist who said, "My heart has heard you say, 'Come and talk with me.' And my heart responds, 'Lord, I am coming'" (Psalm 27:8, NLT). While we are not literally walking the hills together, He is with us all the same.

Reflection

How do you pursue fellowship with Jesus on a daily basis? Do you open God's Word expecting to hear from Him? Think back to a time when you felt the Holy Spirit's prompting; how did you respond? What is one way you could walk more intentionally with Jesus going forward?

"A Bible that's falling apart usually belongs to someone who isn't."

—Charles H. Spurgeon

Day 3

Jesus replied, "My Father is always working, and so am I."

—John 5:17, NLT

Go Looking for Hope

A couple I know has been in battles on many different fronts for years. They've dealt with cancer, discovering that several of their children were victims of sexual assault, financial issues, serious church hurt, a situation with a stalker, and more. There has been immense expense and trouble involved. A job has even been in jeopardy because of the time required to face these battles, not to mention the emotional load.

I don't know about you, but I would probably be curled up in a corner in the fetal position under such a long onslaught! At the very least, it would be hard to find hope.

Yet my friends handled it so differently. They've evidenced a truly joyful spirit. Sure, they get discouraged at times, but then they bounce back to joy. And in the process, we get updates that are simply astounding—incredible things that God is doing. A legal situation looks dire, but God miraculously changes the judge's heart. Connections are made that bring answers on the very day they are needed. Finances arrive out of nowhere that *precisely* match the need. It is miracle after miracle.

Someone asked the wife, "Why is it that your family receives so many miracles from God?"

She replied, "Do we? Or do we just see them when they happen?" As she told me later, "I think miracles happen to all of us every day—it's just a matter of choosing to see them."

In our troubles, it can be so easy to forget this promise from Jesus: "My Father is always working, and so am I." (John 5:17, NLT) *He is always working.* Every day, our default should be to *assume* God is at work in our lives.

What are your troubles? Finances? Health? Relationships? All of the above? In any given day, God's miracles may not—almost certainly will not!—look exactly how we expect. But hope is there because God is there.

God tells us, "Whatever is true, whatever is noble, whatever is right, whatever is pure, whatever is lovely, whatever is admirable—if anything is excellent or praiseworthy—think about such things" (Philippians 4:8). In other words: we must go *looking* for those things that spark hope because they probably won't come looking for us. And as we make that a habit, our eyes will be opened to the ways God is working in our lives every day.

Reflection

Write a prayer to God, thanking Him for always being at work and asking Him to give you eyes to see how He is at work. Then at the end of today, write down some of the tiny "miracles" that blessed your day. Consider making this a daily habit.

"There are only two ways to live your life. One is as though nothing is a miracle. The other is as though everything is a miracle."

—Albert Einstein

Day 4

But truly God has listened; he has attended to the voice of my prayer. Blessed be God, because he has not rejected my prayer or removed his steadfast love from me!

—**Psalm 66:19-20**, ESV

There Is a God . . . And I'm Not Him

The 1993 movie *Rudy* is a true story about a young man who pursues an almost-impossible dream of getting into and playing football for the University of Notre Dame. He doesn't have the grades, he's too small, he has no money, but he maintains an incredible sense of hope. He goes through so much—even being homeless—to pursue his dream. He constantly beseeches God for the answer he wants. And at the final deadline he asks his priest, "Have I prayed enough? Have I done everything I possibly can?" He is basically asking, "How can I *make* God do this thing that I am so desperate for?"

We all have desperate desires. I am desperate for my sweet teenage son to be healed of epilepsy—to be in the category of those who never have a seizure after the age of 19. I have spent so many hours in anguished prayer for this disability that affects everything about his academics and social life to be taken away.

Where are you desperate for a particular answer from God? Maybe you're moving to a new city and need affordable housing. Maybe you are pregnant and worried about a concerning ultrasound. Perhaps you urgently need a caregiver for your aging parents.

We beseech our great big God for these things. We pray and live in desperate hope. We *expect* Him to work, because He loves us. But there is something else we must also do.

As the priest looks at Rudy and what he wants from God so desperately, he replies, "Son, in thirty-five years of religious studies, I have come up with only two hard, incontrovertible facts: there is a God, and I'm not him."

There is a God. And I'm not Him.

If we're going to keep true hope while praying for our desperate desires, we must also have the humility to lay them down. In the end, God is the One who put the stars into motion. He is sovereign, so His answer will prevail . . . and it may not be the same as ours.

Now, sometimes these desperate desires are placed into our heart by God. And Jesus tells us to "keep on asking" and "keep on knocking" on that door! (Matthew 7:7, NLT) But we must also, always, acknowledge to Him that "You are God, and I am not. *Your* will be done."

Reflection

What is one of your most desperate desires? How can you both pursue it in prayer *and* have the humility to tell God, "You are God, and I am not" in this area? In the past, have you ever surrendered a desperate desire to God? If so, what was the result?

"In the light of eternity we shall see that what we desired would have been fatal to us, and that what we would have avoided was essential to our well-being."

—Francois Fenelon

Day 5

Be strong and courageous. Do not be frightened, and do not be dismayed, for the LORD your God is with you wherever you go.

—Joshua 1:9, ESV

Decide on Courage

God had dramatically rescued the Israelites from slavery and led them toward the Promised Land. What would it be like? So much uncertainty—and so much hope. Twelve trusted leaders spied out the land and brought back samples of the astounding bounty; one cluster of grapes required two men to carry!

But ten of these men quenched the people's hope. How? By sparking fear. They spoke of fortified cities guarded by towering men. Compared to them, "we felt like grasshoppers," they said. "They are stronger than we [are]" (Numbers 13:33, 31, NLT).

They were right, of course. The ragtag multitude of men, women, and children was no match for mighty warriors. So they gave in to fear. They wept and complained and rebelled against God by refusing to believe that He was infinitely mightier than the giants of the land.

Our uncertainty can either lead to trust or to fear. And fear is the greatest enemy of hope. I'll speak frankly. Ever since we discovered Luke's epilepsy, uncertainty has hovered over my head and fear has tried to get a foothold in my heart. It is easy to cringe when I see a call come in from Luke's school. *What's happened?* It is easy to hover over my son, to protect (to *overprotect*, if truth be told), to picture fearsome outcomes when he is away on a retreat—or at college.

What areas of uncertainty are you being asked to carry? What big thing are you being tasked with? We cannot fixate on the *obstacles* in the unknown: that builds fear and robs our hope. Instead, listen to God's solution, given to Joshua as a second chance at the Promised Land: "Be strong and courageous!" (Joshua 1:9, NLT).

He is saying, *Decide* to have courage. This is courage based not on feeling, but on taking action in trust. It is based, God says in the rest of that passage, on meditating on His Word, chewing slowly on a small chunk of Scripture and absorbing the nutritive truth. And He reminds us that we are not alone. "The Lord your God is with you wherever you go." We don't drift into the uncertain waters of the future alone, holding a little sticky note with a Bible verse. The actual living God, the epitome of power and peace, goes with us. Fear builds despair. But choosing courage in the Lord brings hope.

Reflection

In what areas of uncertainty might fear be attempting to get a foothold in your life? If you had the feeling of courage instead of fear, what might you be doing differently in those areas? What might help you step out in actions of courage to confront your fear? (One idea: Ask the Lord to give you a Scripture to meditate on that would keep your eyes fixed on Him. Write the Scripture down and post it somewhere to help you dwell on it.)

"Courage is fear that has said its prayers."

—Karle Wilson Baker

Day 6

Now we see things imperfectly, like puzzling reflections in a mirror, but then we will see everything with perfect clarity. All that I know now is partial and incomplete, but then I will know everything completely, just as God now knows me completely.

—1 Corinthians 13:12, NLT

Accept the Mystery

As a kid, my friend Sofia was a mystery junkie. She read every Nancy Drew book, loved playing Clue, and her favorite TV show was *Murder She Wrote*. Just knowing "whodunnit" wasn't enough. She wanted to know the *why*—the motive behind it all.

But a few years ago, she encountered her own mystery. Sofia was faced with a medical condition that, to this day, no one has been able to diagnose. She sought help from multiple doctors. She spent hours online trying to uncover what was behind her symptoms. She consulted with clinical nutritionists and tried a radical diet change.

She desperately wanted to solve this mystery. But no answers came. Finally, she told me:

> "I had to accept that this was just a mystery that God did not have to solve for me. He owed me nothing. Instead, He invited me into the mystery of His sovereignty. He beckoned me to trust Him more with what He *didn't* reveal, as opposed

> to what He *could* reveal. He wanted me to revel in what He revealed about himself in Scripture.
>
> I began to spend more and more time studying Scripture and trying to learn more about His character—because I had to learn to trust His character."

All of us have mysteries. *Why is my child disabled? Why am I still single? Why am I dealing with this pain?* To find hope, we have to learn to trust God's character. And truly, how else can we learn that *except* by walking through mysteries we would never have chosen? As Sofia explained, "I learned that God was faithful no matter what. And that He loves me more than I will ever know. I had to learn to trust His heart when I couldn't trace His hand."

Our finite minds cannot comprehend our infinite God. He sees the full picture, while we only see a few pieces that don't seem to fit together. Sometimes instead of asking "why," we must instead trust that He has a purpose. Maybe He is stretching our faith for a reason we will find out in twenty years. Maybe He is simply drawing us closer to Him. Either way, we must investigate His character and *choose* to trust, accept the mystery, and wait in hope. And maybe, just maybe, we will suddenly discover how He was working, which makes it easier to trust during the next mystery.

Reflection

How is God calling you to trust His heart even when you can't trace His hand? How might meditating on God's character (His love, mercy, wisdom, power, goodness, steadfastness . . .) help you face your unanswered questions? Pick one of His character attributes and write a prayer of meditation, trusting Him in that area.

"God is always doing 10,000 things in your life, and you may be aware of three of them."

—John Piper

Day 7

You have heard that it was said,
"Love your neighbor and hate your enemy."
But I tell you, love your enemies and pray
for those who persecute you, that you
may be children of your Father in heaven.

—Matthew 5:43-45

What Would You Do If You Loved Her?

At a recent marriage event where my husband Jeff and I spoke, a woman I will call Maggie described a hopeless situation she had lived with for years. While her husband was growing up, his mom (Maggie's mother-in-law) had been damagingly critical. As an adult, he was understandably wary of his mother. But Maggie wanted her children to know their grandmother. And she noticed Grandma was softer with the grandkids, although still extremely difficult with Maggie and her husband.

Maggie felt God calling her to love this woman in the way Jesus describes loving our enemies, even though she had no hope anything would change.

After one particularly bad interaction, she angrily said, "I can't love this woman, God!" But she felt God saying, "I don't expect you to love her. Let me love her *through* you." Then she heard this question: "What would you do *if* you loved her?"

Maggie said, "Well, if I loved her, I would call and update her on the grandkids. If I loved her, I would visit her on more than just special occasions. She loves cooking and trying out recipes, so if I loved her, I would show more interest and ask about her favorites."

Instantly, Maggie felt God was saying, "Exactly. Do what you would do if you already loved her."

Maggie began doing those little things. And at first it was hard. ("I didn't *want* to do things like call and chat and ask her for her cinnamon roll recipe!") As she was obedient, though, something happened. Her mother-in-law mellowed a bit. A few positive traits began to peek through the negative ones. Her husband began to see that his mom had character qualities other than "being mean." He realized her manner was likely a signal of a mental illness, for which she needed help. And as he saw her soften, it softened him toward her.

After years of no hope that things could change, things suddenly *were* changing. And it was because Maggie accepted the calling we all have, to love our enemies.

Wherever we feel stuck, hopeless, and angry in a relationship, we have a way to find hope: Be loving and kind, even when it is hard. Be a light in a dark place. In an imperfect world, the actual results are in God's hands . . . but our choice to love is how we can have hope in ours.

Reflection

How do you feel when you read the command, "love your enemy"? What would it look like to allow God to love the hard people in your life through you? How would loving those hard people require you to depend on Him?

"Love does not dishonor others. The way we treat the people we disagree with the most is a report card on our faith."

—Bob Goff

Day 8

Blessed are the pure in heart, for they will see God.

—Matthew 5:8

Be Pure in Heart

In Homer's *Odyssey*, the sirens sang to lure sailors into jumping to their deaths. Odysseus ordered his men to put beeswax in their ears to block the sound. Yet he was curious. He had his men tie him to the ship's mast so he could listen to the alluring sirens' song until they passed the danger.

Many years later, the sirens appeared in another story, *Jason and the Argonauts*. Jason knew the temptation would come. But he handled it very differently. Instead of beeswax and a rope, he brought a skilled harpist onboard. And the harpist played such exceptionally beautiful music that the crew never heard the sirens' songs.

Every day, each of us faces temptations big and little. To snap at our spouse. To read that explicit sex scene. To share the tempting news that really isn't ours to share. To take those office supplies because they'll never be missed. To judge our colleague for leaving her husband. And we feel justified. Or guilty. Or all of the above. Our hope and joy shrivels under the onslaught.

So every day, each of us has two options. We can open ourselves to those temptations out of curiosity or desire, or we can overcome them by filling our hearts and minds with what is pure and beautiful instead. To, as Jesus said, be pure in heart, and see God.

In this journey thus far, you've seen some key factors that are crucial to finding hope—attitudes and habits like love, trust, humility, and keeping an eternal perspective. They are essential. But they will never become real in our lives if we don't actually put in the work each day to build those habits to begin with. To pursue holiness in the face of our sinful desire to compromise. To be obedient to God even when, if we're really honest, we don't want to be. To love Jesus above all else.

We must not tie ourselves to the mast so we can dabble in sin, thinking it won't affect us. Instead, let's do the work to be pure in heart and see God more clearly. Let's listen for His voice in His Word every day so we will always hear it over what the world plays in our ear. And as we *choose* to tune our heart to His voice, the temptations—to snap, lust, gossip, pilfer, judge—will lose their strength as our hearts sing along with hope.

Reflection

In the privacy of this journal space, what temptations have you wanted to dabble in, out of curiosity or desire? What consequences have come into your life as a result? Going forward, what might you do to tune your heart to God's voice and message, so as to turn your heart away from that temptation?

*"The content of
your character
is your choice.
Day by day,
what you choose,
what you think
and what you do
is who you become."*

—Heraclitus

Day 9

Brothers and sisters, we do not want you to be uninformed about those who sleep in death, so that you do not grieve like the rest of mankind, who have no hope.

—1 Thessalonians 4:13

God Is Here Somewhere . . . Seek Him

In 2021, a young Christian woman named Jane Marczewski sang on *America's Got Talent* under the stage name Nightbirde. Everyone was moved by her luminous joy and hope in the face of terminal cancer. Her blog, *God is on the Bathroom Floor*, went viral. It describes how God was there in her hardest moments of sickness when she was lying on her bathroom floor, and it has a powerful lesson for anyone going through suffering.

> I remind myself that I'm praying to the God who let the Israelites stay lost for decades. They begged to arrive in the Promised Land, but instead He let them wander, answering prayers they didn't pray. For forty years, their shoes didn't wear out. Fire lit their path each night. Every morning, He sent them mercy-bread from heaven.
>
> I look hard for the answers to the prayers that I didn't pray. I look for the mercy-bread that He promised to bake fresh for me each morning. The Israelites called it *manna*, which means "what is it?" That's the same question I'm asking—

again, and again. There's mercy here somewhere—*but what is it? What is it? What is it? . . .* It's not the mercy that I asked for, but it *is* mercy nonetheless.

Your pain may be different from Nightbirde's. You might be watching a loved one suffer. Perhaps you wrestle with constant exhaustion, depression, or anxiety. Maybe you worked for many years to build a business, only to be betrayed and forced out.

Believers in Jesus will grieve and suffer because we are human and living in a fallen world. Yet we grieve and suffer differently than all others. Why? We have that eternal perspective we discussed on Day 1: the hope of heaven! Nightbirde wasn't just putting on a brave face: she actually had *joy.* And so can we. The pain is there, but so is God. We know there is mercy here somewhere.

What is the mercy in the moment for you? What glimpse of Jesus can you get right this minute? Where is there a small answer you can grab hold of fiercely?

On February 19, 2022, Jane Marczewski stepped into eternity. When I get to heaven, I'm looking forward to hanging out with this girl. I want to thank her for giving us an example of how to look hard for the answers to prayers we didn't pray.

Reflection

Read Nightbirde's words again, slowly. (You may want to search for and read the entire blog.) How do you feel when you read her words? Does your grief look different than an unbeliever's grief? Read the quote on the next page. What do you need to believe about God to be able to say "thank you" in the face of suffering?

"I learn a new prayer: **thank you.** It's a prayer I don't mean yet, but will repeat until I do."

—Nightbirde

Day 10

Love one another. As I have loved you,
so you must love one another. By this
everyone will know that you are my disciples,
if you love one another.

—John 13:34-35

Loving One Another

Picture saying goodbye to a loved one in the years before easy communication. Your son was going off to war. Or your sister, cousin, or dear friend was about to board a ship across a dangerous ocean. Before that final parting, you would almost certainly try to fit in the most important things you wanted to say. And the last evening would be especially precious.

Jesus probably had those feelings as the time approached for Him to say goodbye. For three years, Jesus lived with, trained, and loved His disciples. These men were His best friends. He was likely grieving the thought of leaving them. And He had something burning in His heart that He wanted to say. Not surprisingly, His message involved the command to love. But more specifically: *to love one another*. Because *that* is how the world would know who these men and women belonged to. *That* is what would draw a watching world to the One who was sacrificing Himself that they might be saved.

This message was so important to Jesus that He humbled himself and washed the feet of His closest friends as an object lesson. It was unheard of for anyone but a servant to wash the dust of the road off of someone else's feet—but that is exactly the point Jesus was trying to make. *Set your rights aside and love and serve one another.*

Two thousand years later, that command to His followers remains. We have lost the practice of foot-washing after hours in sandals on arid dirt roads, so we likely won't have the occasion to humble ourselves and actually wash our fellow believer's dusty feet. But are we willing to bring food, drinks, and sincere smiles to the church meeting when we've been hurt that someone else was asked to be the leader? Are we willing to humble ourselves and set aside our political differences when we think our fellow believer is oh-so-*wrong*? Do we *make* time to be in a small group or Bible study, even when we're busy?

If we are going to find hope in a difficult culture, it will often come through finding strength and fellowship in the family of God. Yes, we live in a world where people are increasingly skeptical of what we believe. But we have each other. As Jesus asked, let us do our part to ensure that a watching world sees a healthy, loving family.

Reflection

Ask yourself: Does my life reflect Christ's command to love and be involved in the lives of other believers? List three ways your life does reflect that—and three ways it does not. Thank God for His grace to continue with the former . . . and for His help to address the latter. What specifically can you do to be part of a healthy, loving family of God?

"Imagine a world where people were skeptical of what we believed but envious of how well we treated one another."

—Andy Stanley

Day 11

And walk in the way of love, just as Christ loved us and gave himself up for us as a fragrant offering and sacrifice to God.

—Ephesians 5:2

Identify with the True Hero

Many of us love superhero movies. The characters put themselves in harm's way, pit themselves against impossible odds to help others, and save the day. It is always very emotional when a beloved character sacrifices him– or herself on behalf of others.

In some of these stories, though, people *revile* the heroes rather than thanking them. My kids were very indignant at that part in *The Incredibles.* Or, in the more grown-up Marvel version, the Avengers just barely prevent the earth's destruction and lose one of their own . . . but the world is furious because innocent lives were lost in the process: *You horrible superheroes! Look at all these people who died! You need to be shut down!*

We viewers indignantly think, *Hold on! These superheroes sacrificed themselves to save you people! Can't you see they are* good*?! It's sad some were lost, but the whole* world *would have been lost without the heroes' sacrifice!*

We defend the superheroes because we are identifying with them. But in real life, we don't do that, do we? When we face trouble or tragedy, we usually identify with the hurt feelings of the angry mob instead. *God, you clearly don't really care! Look at all this tragedy in the world—or in my life! I'm not following a God who would allow that!*

In the movies, the main thing the angry people miss is that these heroes are laying their lives down *for them.* In other words, the heroes have *proved,* over and over, that they are good and people can trust them.

In real life, we might miss that as well.

Friends, let's not do that. Yes, we will have times of trouble or heartbreak in this fallen world. But let's identify with the hero of the story. Let's remember that Jesus laid His life down, enduring a torturous death on behalf of us who all too often get angry at Him. The blood-stained cross demonstrates more than anything else in the universe that our all-powerful God isn't some distant deity who has left us on our own. He is a pursuing God who loves us so much He sacrificed Himself for us. In other words, He has *proved* that He is good, so we can trust Him.

Reflection

Write down five ways that you *know* God is good. How might remembering that truth help you the next time you encounter trouble or tragedy? Put a bookmark on this page, and come back to this list when you encounter trouble or tragedy to remind yourself of what you know of God.

"The maker of the stars would rather die for you than live without you."

—Max Lucado

Day 12

For the word of God is alive and active.
Sharper than any double-edged sword,
it penetrates even to dividing soul and spirit,
joints and marrow; it judges the thoughts
and attitudes of the heart.

—**Hebrews 4:12**

The Word Is Alive

Imagine you are a Special Forces soldier on assignment in a dark and difficult land, working with your team on a dangerous mission to rescue people destined for destruction.

Would there be anything more discouraging than feeling like you were no longer getting instructions and support from your superiors? For soldiers, being in danger is part of the job. But being in danger and *also* feeling abandoned makes it much harder to hold on to courage and hope.

Very little in our world today can make us more sneakily hopeless than the idea that God doesn't still speak to us, that there's no way to know what He would say to us. And sadly, one reason for that hopeless belief today is the concept that we can't *fully* trust the Bible. According to that thought, the Bible was written for a different time and a different culture, so certain teachings of the Bible no longer apply.

The problem is, if we can't trust all of it, we don't know what we can trust. We may not think of it this way, but that is the equivalent of Special Forces soldiers being abandoned because they can no longer get trustworthy communication from their superiors. Why? Because in real life, *we are* Special Forces soldiers who desperately need guidance every day. We are operating in dark and difficult territory—a world under the authority of the evil one (2 Corinthians 4:3-4)—while on assignment for our true king.

Thankfully, our king has not abandoned us. He says His Word is powerful and *living*. In some mysterious way, our commander has given us a communication that is alive and dynamic, not dead and static. And in Jesus, His Word also lives *in* us, changing us.

The great tragedy is how many people view the Bible as static, dead, or written only for a particular time. But if the Word is somehow mysteriously alive, then the Word of God is able to fully guide us today, providing encouragement and support while we do what God has called us to do. We do not have to fumble our way through a battlefield without the guidance of the One who sent us into that battlefield in the first place! We can have the confident hope that He is always there and we should *expect* to hear from Him. And if we are listening, we will.

Reflection

What feels like a battleground right now? Where are you looking for guidance and direction? (Friends? Spouse? Bible studies? Scripture?) No matter where else you seek guidance, plan this week to read the Bible every day and ask God to speak to you about the matter at hand. Journal what happens.

"Our Bible . . .
. . . is not only a book
which was once
spoken, but it is
also a book which
is now speaking."

—A.W. Tozer

Day 13

I remain confident of this: I will see the goodness of the LORD in the land of the living. Wait for the LORD; be strong and take heart and wait for the LORD.

—Psalm 27:13-14

In the Land of the Living

What is the focus of your hope each day? We've pondered the hope of heaven, where all wrongs will be made right, all sorrows wiped away. And that hope is real and certain and glorious. But is it the sum total of biblical hope?

In Psalm 27, David writes in the midst of catastrophe. He's pursued by enemies, he's been lied about and forsaken, he's undergone cruelty and tragedy. David pours out his lament . . . yet amidst these very real agonies he also declares, *"I remain confident of this: I will see the goodness of the LORD in the land of the living."* This is not a future hope for the sweet by and by. David declares that he *will* see the goodness of the Lord right here on planet Earth. He just must take heart and wait for it.

How can David make this declaration—and how can we?

The answer is that we must trust God's character. God *is* goodness; He *is* love! And that gives us certainty that He will keep His promises. His mercies will be new every morning here on earth, not just in heaven (Lamentations 3:22-23).

When we don't believe God is fully good, compassionate, and loving toward us, we don't fully trust Him. But once we accept that these are God's attributes, we will have assurance that His mercy, justice, and kindness will be there for us—not just someday, but right now, wherever we are today.

Grasping the goodness of God is also the antidote to fear. "The LORD is my light and my salvation; whom shall I fear?" David sings. "The LORD is the strength of my life; of whom shall I be afraid?" (Psalm 27:1, NKJV). When we fix our eyes on the manifest goodness of God, courage wells up. Strength and trust are renewed. Hope soars.

I'm so grateful that, through Jesus, we have heaven. Yet I'm also grateful for Jesus' promise that we have a good Father who is with us *right now.* And for His promise of good gifts here on this earth (Matthew 7:11). After all, Jesus is *Immanuel*—God with us on this earth! God with us in the joy and celebration, God with us in the desperate, lonely place. And God with us always, an ever-present help *here*—in time of trouble.

Reflection

Do you try to protect your heart by not hoping for too much from God so you won't be disappointed? How can you both trust your heavenly Father *and* expect to see good things in the land of the living? Write out a prayer of trust and expectation to Him.

"If God is holy,
then He can't sin.
If God can't sin, then
He can't sin against me.
If He can't sin against me,
shouldn't that make Him
the most trustworthy
being there is?"

—Jackie Hill Perry

Day 14

The Lord *himself goes before you*
and will be with you; he will never
leave you nor forsake you.
Do not be afraid; do not be discouraged.

—Deuteronomy 31:8

How Do You Know He Hasn't?

When you're a public speaker, losing your voice is a problem. And in 2019, for the first time in fifteen years, I showed up for a marriage event with complete laryngitis—I could barely whisper. Even worse, although he was able to hide it, Jeff was miserable from a bad cold. We usually lead marriage retreats together, but the entire weekend was going to be on his feverish shoulders.

We had prayed for healing, and our hopes were dashed. I hated Jeff having to carry everything and hated disappointing the attendees and the event organizers, who were close friends. If I'm being really transparent, I was also sad that the retreat center itself was not seeing us at our best, since we'd hoped they might invite us to lead several marriage retreats the next year.

You've probably had hopes dashed, too. You desperately prayed for your restaurant to bring in enough revenue this weekend but it didn't happen. You tried so hard to stay off the layoff list and got the pink slip anyway.

This is often our cry: *Why doesn't God stop these bad things from happening?!*

That disappointing weekend, this thought dropped into my heart: *How do you know He hasn't?*

Suddenly, God brought to mind *fifteen years* of events that had never before been interrupted. I thought of *many* events where I'd been under the weather but had miraculous energy when I walked onstage. With a jolt, I realized that although this situation was awkward, it was happening at a marriage event *for close friends* who would lead attendees to handle it with humor and grace. If this was going to happen, I probably would have *chosen* it to be at this event. (With apologies to our friends!)

How do you know He hasn't? God clearly *has* stopped bad things from happening time and time again in our lives. As I began tallying up the visible ways God had protected us, rather than the ways He hadn't, the list expanded. Perhaps He had prevented things like car accidents, disease, heartbreak, tragedy. Wait . . . *perhaps?* Given that the enemy circles like a roaring lion in order to devour us (1 Peter 5:8), it is almost *certain* that God has prevented a host of devastating problems that we will not know about until heaven.

Guess what happens when we begin thinking on that, friends? The only thing that is dashed is despair! Because gratitude and hope are built.

Reflection

List ten visible ways that you can see God has protected you and your loved ones (e.g., your child got sick, but not until *after* the big test; you didn't make the community choir, but if you had, you wouldn't have been around when your mom needed you). Then, speculate about ten ways God *may* have protected you that you cannot see. What does that do to your outlook? Your trust in Him?

"The root of joy
is gratefulness.
. . . For it is not joy
that makes us
grateful; it is
gratitude that
makes us joyful."

—David Steindl-Rast

Day 15

Dear friends, I warn you as "temporary residents and foreigners" to keep away from worldly desires that wage war against your very souls.

—1 Peter 2:11, NLT

Living as Foreigners

It felt like walking through liquid heat. Soldiering through the sultry days as missionaries in their newly adopted tropical country, Emily and her family sorely missed air conditioning. The fans kept air moving and kept them sane—until daily power outages rendered the fans useless. Mosquitoes feasted on their flesh, laundry wouldn't dry in the relentless humidity, and they were irritable from the constant discomfort.

But then a package arrived at the post office. The promise of news and goodies from home buoyed Emily's outlook. Kids in tow, she stood in the long line, cheerful expectation bolstering her patience. As she finally got to the counter, the postal worker said "Sorry, we're closed for the day," and shut the window.

Her shock catapulted into outrage, which she was sorely tempted to vent. Were they treating her this way just because she was a foreigner?

And that's when she remembered why they had come here. The beautiful people in this remote city were largely without eternal hope. She was indeed a foreigner—and was called to live differently so those around her would see the One she represented. She resolved to reflect the joy of Jesus despite the difficulties.

The thing is, as followers of Jesus, we are *all* foreigners in a world that is not our home. And in this world we represent not ourselves but Him. So when responding to that unfair colleague or the *totally* inaccurate person on social media, God asks us to reflect His love rather than our irritation, His grace rather than our oh-so-rightness.

Friends, it can be hard to live away from our heavenly home. We must look for glimpses of eternity, encouragement in an arduous journey. And one key way to do that is to see ourselves as we really are: bearers of the hope of eternity in this world. We are those who stretch out His glorious treasure to those around us.

Yes, the ruler of this dark realm will resist our efforts, and we will experience troubles and tragedy. But we can carry on because our eternal hope is sure in Jesus. Nothing in this world can touch it. Let's persevere with prayer and in the power of the Holy Spirit, dispensing the hope of Christ, aching that others will be caught up in the joy of Jesus and join the ranks of those who are homesick for a place we haven't yet seen.

Reflection

Consider how you tend to speak and act when difficulties hit. Thinking of yourself as an ambassador of Christ, what specifically might you be called to handle differently? How can you remind yourself that this world is not your home? Is there someone you can pray for or befriend, inviting them into the eternal hope of journeying with Jesus?

"If I find in myself a desire which no experience in this world can satisfy, the most probable explanation is that I was made for another world."

—C. S. Lewis

Day 16

The LORD drove the sea back with a strong east wind. . . .
The waters were divided, and the Israelites went through the sea on dry ground, with a wall of water on their right and on their left.

—Exodus 14:21-22

Sometimes We Can't Predict the Rescue

We love watching action-movie characters come up against impossible odds and experience miraculous rescues. A tree breaks their fall when they jump. A helicopter rushes in. They clip the wires seconds before the bomb explodes.

The Israelites faced their own real-life impossible odds, escaping from Pharoah and slavery. They were running for their lives, chased by Pharoah's army toward the Red Sea. There was nowhere for them to go. They and their children were sure to be captured, killed by the soldiers, or drown.

They must have felt utterly hopeless.

But what happened? God parted the sea! Walls of water suddenly began to rise up on either side, forming a path of escape. What?! I'll bet not one of them, in their fear of impending death or capture, prayed, "Oh, God, it would be great if You could just part the sea. You know, create a path for us to cross safely. Yes, that seems like the best plan for saving us right now."

No one could've predicted that type of rescue. Yet God knew. This was a way His glory could be displayed, while rescuing those He loved.

As we read this story, it is easy to mentally skip through because we know what happens. God's people are chased . . . yada yada . . . Red Sea and Pharoah's army . . . the waters part and they are saved. It is like watching a chase scene in a movie we have seen many times—we know what to expect.

But those real people in their real time of desperation had no hope. The rescue was miraculous and unexpected and completely God's idea.

When we are in a time of desperation, we may feel hopeless. Or maybe we try to trust but also have the rescue plan all worked out. Just do this, God, okay? Just bring a bonus check so I can pay that debt. Just ensure the surgery worked. Just tell my husband to stop being so stubborn. Our goal is to avoid struggle or pain. And sometimes God does answer our prayers in the specific ways we ask. But often His plan is so much bigger.

Let's remember that we don't really want Him to give us what we want—we want to see the walls of water rising up on either side.

Reflection

Is there a situation that appears hopeless to you right now? What can you do to remind yourself that God is working and has a plan that may look nothing like you could have imagined?

"I don't believe God allows surrendered hearts to continue to long for things He will not ultimately grant in one way or another. Our disappointment with God is often the result of our small thinking."

—Beth Moore

Day 17

Therefore, since we have such a hope,
we are very bold.

—2 Corinthians 3:12

Stuck in the Elevator

Fiona was claustrophobic. So imagine her fear when, in a packed elevator, the doors wouldn't open. Face-to-face with her ten-year-old son—and twelve strangers—she knew something was drastically wrong. The elevator being stuck was only the beginning. Very quickly, as passengers pushed buttons and called for help, she could sense they were on the verge of panic and anger. She was, too.

Since they were packed in so tightly, Fiona felt, rather than heard, the sharp intake of whimpering breaths from the woman next to her, who was holding a one-year-old baby. Fiona closed her eyes and prayed, *Oh God, help me to stay calm.*

In that moment, she had to face the same decision all of us must make when fear coils itself around our hearts: Succumb to the fear or step up. Fiona realized, *God has me here for a reason. I think I'm supposed to help this volatile group of people stay calm.* Purpose chased out panic. So she smiled at the terrified woman and asked—as if it were Fiona's greatest pleasure—to hold the baby. The woman handed over her daughter with relief.

Fiona started looking people in the eye and smiling. She suggested they go around and introduce themselves. She prayed, *Dear Lord, if something is going to be contagious in this tiny, cramped space, let it be hope.*

And slowly things lightened. There was a bit of laughter. They passed around gum, and Fiona fed the baby a bottle. They were in this together. Instead of panic, an unexplained, supernatural peace descended. The act of sharing candy, water bottles, and reassurance almost felt like breaking bread and passing wine.

Finally, the elevator started moving and the doors opened. Firefighters and EMS workers lined the lobby with gurneys, clearly expecting many panicked people in need of medical attention. Instead, each of the fourteen people walked past with smiles and thanks. When Fiona's son said he was never getting in an elevator again, Fiona stopped him. "Don't miss what happened here. That was *holy.*" Where there could've been destructive anger and fear, there was civility and community.

In our times of distress and fear, purpose chases out panic. God can use *one* person to turn a tide. Just like when, in an elevator filled with trembling people, the Holy Spirit worked the (very small) room and filled it with hope.

Reflection

What is a situation you face where you are
tempted to be overcome by fear?
Pray now—and then—for God to replace
your fear with faith. When you feel fear
preying upon your resolve, what sense
of purpose can help you move past the panic?

"The remarkable thing about fearing God is that when you fear God you fear nothing else, whereas if you do not fear God you fear everything else."

—Oswald Chambers

Day 18

And if you search for him with all your heart and soul, you will find him.

—Deuteronomy 4:29, NLT

Stopped at the Bedroom Door

Most of us have nonstop lives. I'm often running to research meetings, flying on airplanes, having long calls with my college-student daughter about projects or job interviews, finding time to connect with my husband, driving to doctor's appointments. . . . All of us are just busy.

So in my own life, I've found that my best chance to get time with God is in the morning, immediately after I've showered and dressed, before I head down to my home office. If I don't take time to sit on my bed and read my Bible before I walk out the bedroom door, I know that no matter how well-intentioned I am ("I'll just return that email and come right back upstairs"), my chances of getting to it are slim.

Not long ago, I went through a challenging season on a book deadline, and my time with God suffered. I knew I needed to be more purposeful, but there was just so much to *do!* One busy morning, I dressed for a big meeting and was about to run downstairs. As I approached the doorway, I felt like I got the spiritual equivalent of an electric jolt. It was as if God was saying, *You know what's going to happen if you walk through that door and go downstairs.*

Part of me wanted to pretend I hadn't heard that. But in that moment, I realized that what came next was going to be purely a choice: was I going to keep going because I didn't want to be late for the meeting? Or was I going to take some time—even just five or ten minutes—to read my Bible and pray?

I realized that my relationship with God was getting distant because I was getting lazy. Ouch. I took off my shoes, climbed up on my bed, and grabbed my Bible and journal.

Our time with God and developing a meaningful relationship with Him will always be a *decision*—even though your quiet time might look very different than mine. (In my book *Find Peace*, I describe a young mom who can never get a "quiet" time but sits with her Bible and has *loud time* with the Lord, surrounded by kids and chaos!) Whatever our life situation is, we need to be intentional about pursuing God. To find hope, we have to find *Him* . . . every day.

Reflection

Do you need to be more purposeful about pursuing God? What changes might be needed in order to make time with God a higher priority in your life and in your day? Write those here, and pick one thing to do differently.

"We serve a God who is waiting to hear from you, and He can't wait to respond."

—Priscilla Shirer

Day 19

Kind words are like honey—sweet to the soul
and healthy for the body.

Proverbs 16:24, NLT

To Have Hope, You Must Be Kind

I have a sweet tooth. I find the best treats are the ooey-gooey kind where you have to lick your fingers afterwards.

Honey is one of those; after you put it on your toast, everything in the vicinity suddenly feels sticky, right? Well, kindness is sort of like that. You put a dab of kindness in the world and the sweetness spreads.

The opposite is also true—when unkindness seeps out in our actions and attitudes, it affects everyone around us. Unkindness sours the atmosphere of our world and our relationships.

The problem is, we don't realize just how often that happens. We value kindness and are blind to our little attitudes of exasperation, negativity, gossip, or frustration. Talking with our girlfriends, we roll our eyes about our husband. We exasperatedly ask our child, "what were you thinking?!" We text our office friend the news that our arrogant coworker was reprimanded: "What goes around comes around!"

And as we do those things, does our sense of hope for the future increase? Or diminish?

We all know the answer.

Unkindness is incompatible with hope. One gives life; the other brings death—to those around us and to us. That's surely one reason kindness is commanded throughout Scripture.

We are always going to be imperfect people. But if we want to have a hopeful outlook rather than a negative one, we must fight our unkind tendencies. And the best method is not to just grit our teeth and try to *not* be negative; it is to actively be kind. To praise others. To express gratitude. To be generous.

One of my favorite research projects involved creating the 30-Day Kindness Challenge. Participants picked someone they wanted a better relationship with, and each day for thirty days they did these three things: They said nothing negative or unkind about their person (either to them or about them to somebody else), they praised their person (to them and someone else), and they did a small action of kindness for them.

Fully 89 percent of relationships improved, with hope being restored for hopeless marriages, parents reconciling with children, and conflicted colleagues suddenly enjoying working together. Why such a dramatic uptick in hope? Because kindness is "sweet to the soul." It impacts us first. It builds our hope and belief that things can indeed change. And as our hope grows, it becomes self-perpetuating as we spread that sticky sweetness to the world around us.

Reflection

Is there a relationship in your life that is causing you to struggle with hope? You want to enjoy your daughter-in-law, your colleague, or that guy you've been dating, but it's been feeling more and more rough. What is one way you might have been unkind to that person without realizing it? How might you counteract that and share sweet words of praise instead? Is there someone for whom you might do the 30-Day Kindness challenge? (If so, go to jointhekindnesschallenge.com.)

"A single act of kindness throws out roots in all directions, and the roots spring up and make new trees."

—Amelia Earhart

Day 20

Rejoice always, pray continually, give thanks in all circumstances; for this is God's will for you in Christ Jesus.

—1 Thessalonians 5:16-18

Giving Thanks in All Things

I was lying on the table, trembling. In the months since learning I had breast cancer, I had been poked and prodded more than I thought possible. It was caught early, but still involved many biopsies, treatments, radiation, disruptions to my schedule, and quite a bit of fear. Not so much a fear of dying, but of pain. I am a wimp when it comes to pain and needles. And now pain and needles seemed like an everyday occurrence. Then a routine OBGYN visit discovered something abnormal. *Great. Just great.* So there I was on the table, needing another painful biopsy, grappling with fear.

Suddenly the Scripture from my morning devotional came to mind. First Thessalonians 5:16-18 says to give thanks in all circumstances. Which meant I needed to give thanks for *this*. It completely took me aback as I was waiting for the doctor to walk in. I realized there *were* actually things to be thankful for.

I had been focused on the pain of the test, but I began telling God, *Thank You, God, that this test even exists! Thank You for the medical community's skill in stopping small problems from becoming big ones. Thanks for being with me. Thanks for drawing me closer to You rather than farther away.*

I realized that in challenging times, we usually focus on all the things to *not* give thanks for, but we can make a conscious choice to turn worry into worship. We can choose to say, *yes, the enemy meant this for evil, but God can turn it to good.* And one of the greatest "goods" is the precious opportunity to see God come close.

Not long ago, a pastor asked how my health was doing. He said his brother had cancer too—a very serious type. His brother had recently said he was *grateful* for this time in his life. Shocked, the pastor exclaimed, "But you could die!"

His brother responded, "Sure. But because of going through this, I have seen Jesus so clearly and so closely. I honestly don't know that I would change it."

Something miraculous happens when we choose to give thanks in *all things*. We suddenly see a bigger picture, and it feeds our hope. Even though it's something we wouldn't have chosen going in, I agree with that pastor's brother. I'm not sure I would change a thing.

Reflection

What is something in your life that you might be inclined to complain about, that you could instead make the conscious choice to be grateful for? How can you use this challenge as an opportunity to see Jesus up close?

"There is power in our choice. When we choose [to be grateful], we decide whether or not the power of gratitude will be permitted to work out hope within us."

—Mercy Multiplied blog

Day 21

And let us not neglect our meeting together,
as some people do, but encourage one another,
especially now that the day of his return is drawing near.

—Hebrews 10:25, NLT

Being Together

Many of us have had moments of doubt and disconnect in our walk of faith. Not long ago, I had lunch with an old friend who was in one of those seasons. Her prayer life was dry. She was drawn to social media groups of those deconstructing their beliefs. She felt a bit distant and downcast. She didn't like it but didn't have much hope things would change. She said, "That is just where I am right now."

I love this friend. And because we trust each other, I felt I could share my heart. I looked across the little café table and asked, "Are you going to church each week?"

There was a pause. "Not really. I got out of the habit during that year I traveled so much for business."

Friends, we have to be willing to be honest with ourselves. As I once heard a pastor say, "If you are going through a season of doubt, ask yourself if you are regularly in corporate worship."

The COVID–19 pandemic showed us many things, and one of them was how easily we could build a habit of going to church virtually rather than in person . . . or not at all. After the world opened up, it was just so comfortable to continue to log in to church in my pajamas. The online option was just *easier.*

And yet God calls us to "meet together." As in . . . *together.* In person.

Not everyone will be able to physically gather for corporate worship, but for those who can, why is it important? The Bible says it is a crucial way to build hope! And a crucial way to encourage one another in times of trial or uncertainty. In some mysterious way, God does a deep work in our hearts as we gather to worship, absorb teaching, and fellowship with others. Watching others raise their hands in adoration of God bolsters our own faith. Listening to the sermon side by side helps us feel less alone. Taking communion together is a sacrament through which we are given strength and remembrance of Jesus. We *need* to come together regularly.

When we have gotten out of the habit of gathering, it may take a month or two of discipline to overcome the temptation to stay home. But God will honor that choice, and soon gathering together will become our new habit, one that continually injects life and encouragement as we fight the good fight of faith.

Reflection

If you are physically able, are you in the habit of weekly, in-person, corporate worship? If so, identify three ways God uses that in your life, and thank Him for them. If you are out of that habit, identify three ways it might be costing you. Write a prayer asking for God's help and strength in developing a new habit, and commit to it.

"Faith development is not about doing the amazing things occasionally but the simple things consistently."

—Mo Huggins

Day 22

And I sent messengers to them, saying, "I am doing a great work and I cannot come down. Why should the work stop while I leave it and come down to you?"

—**Nehemiah 6:3**, ESV

Do Not Come Down

Ages ago, I was a newspaper columnist on hot-button cultural issues. I was tasked with bringing my perspective as a Christian wife and mom to a weekly debate with a woman who was single, progressive, and agnostic.

While I felt called to the job, it was challenging. I was constantly flooded with horrible emails and comments. People didn't just disagree with my beliefs, they brutally shredded me personally. (One classic: "How can I respect anything you're saying when you are so overweight?") My stomach churned; it became difficult to concentrate. I was constantly thinking, *What are they saying about me now?*

Finally, my husband, Jeff, stepped in, saying, "Please stop reading your column emails and comments. Trust me to read them—and only show you what I think you need to see." His kindness protected me and helped train me in something vital to my future ministry. I learned how to not get trapped by what others think so I can stay focused on what God called me to. Mostly.

Is there some mission that you are being distracted from because you're listening to what other people say? Nehemiah's story is instructive. The Jews had returned from Babylonian exile to a Jerusalem in ruins, under dire threat from their enemies. Nehemiah led the men to rapidly rebuild the wall around the city while also protecting it. They wielded both swords and trowels. But Nehemiah was also constantly being pestered by opponents and even supposed allies. They kept trying to stir up controversy. And asking him to come down from the wall and deal with such-and-such.

Nehemiah saw what we also need to see: some people are just toxic, and engaging with them is a trap. (Trolls on social media, anyone?) He said he was doing a great work and wasn't going to engage. He wasn't even going to bother listening to the trolls, much less respond.

Being on mission means staying laser focused. Otherwise our hope gets sucked away and we get tempted to give up. But our heart clears and hope rises as we refuse to be distracted by worrying about (or responding to) what other people say, and instead watch our great God guiding us in our calling. As we see Him working, *of course* we aren't going to stop building the wall! Because our hope is not based on other people's opinions but on the One who led us to the wall in the first place.

Reflection

In what ways are you like or unlike Nehemiah? Are there ways you've allowed the opinions of others to steal your hope and distract you from what God has for you? What can you do to stay "on mission" and not allow that distraction?

"One of Satan's cleverest attacks is getting us to pour our time and energy into people who resent the grace we share and who will never change, keeping us from spending time with and focusing on others whom we can love and serve."

—Gary Thomas

Day 23

Therefore, if anyone is in Christ, [s]he is a new creation.
The old has passed away; behold, the new has come.

—2 Corinthians 5:17, ESV

Nurturing Our New Nature

You're lying in bed at 3:00 a.m., wide awake. The rent is due on Friday, your husband's contract job ended, and a flood of bills are coming due—bills your part-time income won't cover. Should you go full-time? Who will watch your boys when they aren't at school so your husband can continue his job search? And how can you encourage him, now that he's so discouraged that he may not *want* to search anymore?

You may have a different circumstance than the one I just described, but who hasn't lain in bed with heart and mind racing? It can feel impossible to stop our anxious thoughts.

This is the opposite of hope and is not God's plan for how we spend our days or nights. We need to look to a simple but deep truth: As a new creation in Christ, an anxious person is not who we are. And fearful thoughts are not the fruit of who we are!

Instead of surrendering to the old nature, God tells us what fruit grows as we cultivate our new nature: "[L]ove, joy, peace, patience, kindness, goodness, faithfulness, gentleness, and self-control." (Galatians 5:22-23, ESV). Those are the characteristics of the Holy

Spirit who lives in us. Fear at 3:00 a.m. is a characteristic of the old nature; being at peace should be the default of the new.

Easy to say, right? I get how challenging this is. So how can we make the fruits of the Spirit our default? *The old nature has to die.* We have to stop feeding it. And we *can.* Romans 6:6-7 says our old selves have been crucified with Him and we are no longer slaves to sin—and that includes distrustful fear. When we worry, we're not trusting God and are putting our hope in our own ability to figure things out. We must fuel the new nature instead—for example, by *choosing* to allow God to handle it all and switching each anxious thought to one of trust.

Surrendering to our new nature doesn't mean we won't ever need additional help (for example, from a pastor or counselor). But as much as we can, let's ***not*** surrender to those anxious "old nature" temptations when they arise. Instead, each time we get that flicker of worry, let's ask the Holy Spirit to grow His characteristics in us and enjoy the increasing joy (and love, peace, patience, etc.) that come as a result.

Reflection

What are some practical ways you can create the default of being at peace when you feel anxious? (For example, identify a verse to help you remember how loved you are by your heavenly Father to help you trust Him—perhaps Isaiah 43:1-4; Romans 8:14-16; or Romans 8:26-27—and memorize it or write it on a card to keep by your bed at night.)

"It's not your job to figure out how God's going to provide. It's your job to ask."

—Rick Warren

Day 24

"Sir," they said, "always give us this bread."
Then Jesus declared, "I am the bread of life. Whoever comes to me will never go hungry, and whoever believes in me will never be thirsty."

—John 6:34-35

He Works When We Are Weary

Are you running on empty because of a demanding schedule that never lets up? Your to-do list is probably filled with worthy things like caring for your family or working hard to meet a deadline. Even the most energetic among us can grow weary. And when our tank runs dry, our spirit becomes depleted and hope dries up like a parched desert tumbleweed.

Jesus' disciples likely felt this way too. In Luke 9:1-6, Jesus sent them out for the first time to do the hard work of ministry. These men hit the ground running, going "from village to village, proclaiming the Good News and healing people everywhere" (Luke 9:6). And when the disciples returned after weeks of exhilarating but exhausting ministry, Jesus took them away to Bethsaida to try to rest.

Here's where the story hits home for us: their work followed them. Crowds of needy people found them and pressed in, demanding their time, energy, and service. Eventually, the crowds became restless and hungry—and the disciples were probably feeling spent, hopeless, and inadequate. There was no way they could feed all these people! Especially with the meager rations of one little boy's lunch—five loaves of bread and two fish.

But Jesus did something amazing that day: He fed everyone. And who was the miracle primarily for? Thousands of people were spread over a wide area, which probably means most of them didn't see the actual miracle. Many probably assumed the disciples brought the food with them.

Although word of the miracle spread afterward, I wonder if Jesus' immediate intention was primarily to encourage His weary disciples. Imagine how reinvigorated and encouraged they were as they witnessed Jesus' power and provision! He was also showing them something we all need to learn: We are trying to accomplish what Jesus has given us to do, but the task is not ours to accomplish in our own strength.

We must not simply marvel at the miracle meal and miss the underlying message. When we are tired, discouraged, and hungry for fresh hope and strength, let's confidently draw near to Jesus, the Bread of Life, giving Him our loaves and fishes and *expecting* that He will work. He promises to do "immeasurably more than all we ask or imagine, according to his power that is at work within us" (Ephesians 3:20). And when His miracle supply flows into our impossible challenge, joy and hope overflow.

Reflection

In what specific area are you weary and in need of Jesus' strength and supply today? Like the disciples, is there a need you believe is yours to fill that Jesus is asking you to lay at His feet? Pray and ask God to show you three ways that He *is* working. Note those here, and add to the list as you see Him work more in the future.

"God's work done in God's way will never lack God's supply."

—Hudson Taylor

Day 25

For through the Spirit we eagerly await by faith the righteousness for which we hope. For in Christ Jesus neither circumcision nor uncircumcision has any value. The only thing that counts is faith expressing itself through love.

—Galatians 5:5-6

Know Who Is Enough

Our culture comes at us with a paradox: It comforts us with coffee mugs and T-shirts that proclaim, "You Are Enough." But at the same time, it pushes long work weeks, impossible beauty standards, and constant images in which we come up short.

Think about that feeling: "I'm not sure I am enough after all." Dreadful, right? Well, under the surface, that's what lingers under every religious belief system except Christianity. In the end, all other faiths say your shot at eternity is all about what you do, how well you do it, and whether you're good enough. Followers of these faiths are always working and striving, never knowing whether they will come up short.

By contrast, the follower of Jesus knows the truth: It is not about what I do, but about what God has already done. There is *nothing* that I can do to earn God's love. He offers salvation as a gift.

Picture the person who loves and serves because they feel they must work their way to God. Now, picture the Christ follower who loves and serves because of their incredible gratitude for what God has already done. Which of the two has more hope?

If we don't always feel hope and joy, we must ask: how often are we sabotaging it because we are still trying to "be enough"?! Maybe we are trying to be a "good enough person" to meet God's standards for heaven. Maybe we are simply trying to feel better about ourselves; if we could just get down to our goal weight, meet our sales targets, or get that acceptance letter . . .

First-century Christians tried to rely on their own "enoughness" too. And Paul challenged them to stop living under the burden and delusion that being a good person and following the rules would accomplish anything. All that matters is a genuine faith in the One who already accomplished everything.

Are you squashing your hope by striving to earn what has already been given? Are you trying to feel better about yourself because you're a good person, hit your sales targets, or look fantastic these days? Even more important, are you trying to have faith in yourself and be your own master? If so, God is calling you to surrender your life to Him and embrace the incredible truth that brings hope and freedom: *It is Jesus who is enough!*

Reflection

In what ways are you trying to be "good enough" for God? To feel better about yourself? Have you ever grappled with the truth that none of us will ever be "good enough" for God—and that He has already accomplished everything that needs to be accomplished? Have you ever accepted His freely-offered love? If not, please consider His offer; He is longing for you to accept Him! One good place to start is www.cru.org, on the link called "How to Know God."

If you are ready, write your prayer of acceptance to God. Then plug in to a Bible-believing church so you can connect with people who will help you grow. If you have previously accepted His salvation, write a prayer to the Lord asking for His help to stop striving and instead rest in the love you have already received.

"Once a man is united to God, how could he not live forever?"

—C. S. Lewis

Day 26

Do not conform to the pattern of this world, but be transformed by the renewing of your mind. Then you will be able to test and approve what God's will is—his good, pleasing and perfect will.

—Romans 12:2

Feed Your Spirit Well

I'm a Diet Coke person. It can be a problem. It's a bit of a joke among my team members—when an event organizer asks, "Is there anything specific we should have on hand for Shaunti?" my team will say, "She will want Diet Coke, but give her water!"

Water is much healthier for my body than Diet Coke, so I'm trying to drink more of one and cut back on the other. We all know that for our bodies to work right, we should try to avoid inputs that could be damaging and instead consume things that are healthy.

We need to do the same thing for our spirits.

When we struggle with worry, stress, or anxiety, we need to examine what sort of mental, emotional, and spiritual inputs we're absorbing.

Just as I really enjoy Diet Coke, I really enjoy reading political news. It takes me back to my "roots" of working on Capitol Hill and stimulates something in me.

The problem is, what it stimulates often isn't healthy. I read an article about what I think is a really harmful policy, and what rises in me is anger and indignation. I listen to bickering television commentators and mentally make points about what someone *should* have said. I get an "insider" email newsletter about what is *really* going on behind the scenes and compulsively follow the links.

I'm flooding my spirit with the equivalent of empty calories at best, and toxic chemicals at worst. Just like my Diet Coke, I may enjoy it, but it sure isn't healthy to absorb too much of it. And I need to be far more purposeful about seeking what brings *life* to my spirit instead: watching uplifting shows, gathering with Christian friends, reading books with great stories or encouraging truths, being in the Word, and listening for God's still, small voice.

What are you tempted to absorb into your spirit that is empty at best and damaging at worst? What do you need to absorb instead? Your temptations may be different from mine, but any damaging inputs are likely stimulating worry, stress, and anxiety in your heart.

Nourishing our spirit requires effort. We are asked to guard our hearts and be discerning and self-disciplined about what we take in and allow to influence us.

If we want to have hope, we need to feed ourselves hope!

Reflection

What are you tempted to absorb that might be toxic to your spirit? Think about your daily inputs—books, social media, news, entertainment, music, conversations. . . . Pray for a few minutes and ask God what inputs you should change in order to build hope.

"You don't have to attend every argument you're invited to."

—Author Unknown

Day 27

The weapons we fight with are not the weapons of the world.
On the contrary, they have divine power to demolish strongholds.

—2 Corinthians 10:4

Kicking Satan Where It Hurts

A few years ago, a group of teenage boys learned that one of their childhood friends had died—and it appeared to be a death of hopelessness. The boys were sad, but also furious. They knew the real cause of that hopelessness. One said, "I hate Satan. I want to kick him where it hurts."

As odd as it might sound, his reaction pointed toward something vital for building hope. Hopelessness often stems from feelings of helplessness. And many of us feel helpless and angry in the face of the evil in this world. It feels as though there is nothing we can do when a sister falls desperately ill, the husband of a dear friend abandons her for another woman, or a hurricane decimates our neighborhood. Our hope falters.

Friends, we are not helpless! Our struggles in this world are "not against flesh and blood, but against . . . the spiritual forces of evil in the heavenly realms" (Ephesians 6:12). We are in a battle, but are only helpless when we do not step into our calling to take up arms.

So how do we do that? We do what that passage in Ephesians 6 says to do! Regardless of what God ultimately decides, we fervently "pray in the Spirit" for our sister to be healed. We "put on the full armor of God" and become a messenger of peace to our grieving friend or devastated neighbors. But more than anything, *we follow hard after God*. We fall in love with Jesus and allow His love to shine out of us to others. *That* is how we kick Satan where it hurts.

James the brother of Jesus explained, "Submit yourselves, then, to God. Resist the devil, and he will flee from you. Come near to God and he will come near to you" (James 4:7-8). Our God has already won the ultimate war. We win the battle when we allow Him to turn hurts into healing, messes into a message of God's goodness, and a test into a testimony. Revelation 12:11 says: "They have defeated [Satan] by the blood of the Lamb *and by their testimony"* (NLT, emphasis mine).

Do you want to walk in hope? To stand strong in the spiritual battle? To overcome evil with good? No matter what, keep following our great God, and encourage others to do the same.

Reflection

Is there a situation in your life or the life of a loved one that is making you really angry at the enemy? How might your determination to pray and follow God with your whole heart actually bring change to that situation? To you? To the Kingdom?

"Prayer is the portal that brings the power of heaven down to earth. It is kryptonite to the enemy and to all his ploys against you."

—Priscilla Shirer

Day 28

Do not get drunk on wine, which leads to debauchery.
Instead, be filled with the Spirit.

—Ephesians 5:18

Under the Influence

In this devotional, we've pondered taking actions that, in our own power, might seem impossible or fearful. And there are so many more examples. Can we really love that unlovable colleague who constantly undermines us? Is it really possible, as a wife and working mom, to step out and pursue that college degree? Can we forgive the drunk driver who brought tragedy to our family?

My friend faced such a challenge when she was shattered by her husband's infidelity. He was shattered too. He knew how horribly he had betrayed her and God. After a year of counseling and separation, his repentance *seemed* genuine, but how could she know? He was doing things to earn back trust, but *could* she trust him?

Some friends said to give him a chance. Others said he was playing her. Or he would never really be able to change.

My friend began praying. A lot. She was still confused and hurt, but she began feeling God was asking her to reconcile. To allow herself to hope. To trust that God could make her husband a new man.

She didn't know if she could do it. And if she could . . . *how*?

The apostle Paul provides a clue for all of us: "Do not get drunk on wine. . . . Instead, be filled with the Spirit." It is an intentional comparison. After all, during Pentecost the early church was so "under the influence" of the Holy Spirit that being drunk is what they were accused of! (Acts 2:13).

Pastor Jeff Norris describes why that comparison matters. "If we are drunk, we do things we wouldn't otherwise do, right? We say things we wouldn't normally say. And we risk things we wouldn't otherwise risk. It's the same when we are filled with the Spirit: We do things we wouldn't otherwise do; say things we wouldn't normally say; and risk things we wouldn't otherwise risk—to the glory of God."

When we are called to do something that we wouldn't otherwise do, we must be filled with the Holy Spirit, not with ourselves and our own trepidation. God will give us His power and use us in ways that do not come naturally.

That is what my friend did. She put boundaries in place, then chose to risk something she wouldn't normally risk: her heart. Today, their marriage is restored—in large part because she decided to be "under the influence."

Reflection

Think of a time when you felt there was something you needed to do that you did not want to do—but you did it anyway. Might that prompt have been from the Holy Spirit? How can you encourage yourself to take a similar step next time?

"Christianity is not simply a body of truth to be believed; it is a supernatural life that is meant to be lived."

—Crawford Loritts

Day 29

They worshiped together at the Temple each day, met in homes for the Lord's Supper, and shared their meals with great joy and generosity—all the while praising God and enjoying the goodwill of all the people. And each day the Lord added to their fellowship those who were being saved.

—Acts 2:46-47, NLT

Not an Island

Friends from grad school recently moved near us in Atlanta. We had always lived across the country, so we were thrilled we would finally be able to hang out. I spent a day apartment hunting with the wife and was stunned to discover that hanging out might be more complicated than we thought. Not one of the modern 2– or 3–bedroom apartments had a floor plan that allowed space for a kitchen or dining room table. The space was instead taken by a large island with four stools lined up side by side.

My friend asked each property manager to be shown a floor plan with space for a table. One broke the news that such a thing didn't exist. "But," we asked, shocked, "how do people have friends over for a meal? How do they have family dinners together?"

"I guess that just doesn't happen much today. And since there's been no demand for such a layout, developers stopped building them."

What a sad trend!

It is ironic that in 1624 the English cleric John Donne observed that, "No man is an island." We are *created* for community. We are not made to do life alone. Yet we can easily get out of the habit of fellowship and into the habit of a quick meal at the kitchen island before dashing off to the next thing.

It is hard to have hope when you're on an island, by yourself.

One of the most appealing things about the early church was how regularly they shared meals together—a picture not just of friendship but of gladness and hope. The watching world *wanted* that, and floods of people were saved. Think about what hope it will bring those who feel isolated to be invited to your home for dinner. Think about what hope it will bring *you* to be purposeful about fellowship.

As our friends searched for an apartment, they decided that no matter what, they *would* find a place that had room for a kitchen table so they could have friends over. It took a while, but they found one. And hanging out with them has been such a source of life for us ever since.

God's design is for us to do life together. So no matter the size of your kitchen, be purposeful about fellowship. We are not meant to be an island.

Reflection

How are you currently intentional about fellowship? What keeps you from pursuing it? What is one thing you can do today that would move you a step closer to fellowship and community?

"No man is an island, entire of itself; every man is a piece of the continent, a part of the main."

—John Donne

Day 30

Oh, magnify the LORD *with me,*
and let us exalt his name together! . . .
Those who look to him are radiant,
and their faces shall never be ashamed.

—Psalm 34:3, 5, ESV

Magnify Him

The Hubble Space Telescope can see as far as 13.4 billion light-years away and has revealed many wonders of the universe. Without the ability to magnify what is beyond our sight, we would be limited to knowing only what our human eyes can see.

The Bible talks about "magnifying" the Lord, meaning that our actions, words, and attitudes should make God more clearly known to others—and ourselves. In us and through us, God's wonders should be seen in a way they may not have been seen otherwise.

Not long ago, Jeff and I had a disagreement that left me with lingering hurt feelings. Normally I don't stew in resentment, but in this case I was struggling to get past being upset with him. It was a Sunday morning, so we drove to church in frosty silence. I ensured the kids sat between us so I wouldn't rub elbows with him.

During worship, we sang the great song, "Christ Be Magnified" by Cody Carnes. We all loved it, so it was playing on the drive home as I reverted back to my mad-at-Jeff bubble.

Suddenly, I felt like God quietly dropped this question into my heart: *Are you magnifying Me by holding on to your hurt against Jeff?*

Sigh.

The answer was more than obvious.

Friends, in the Bible we are encouraged, over and over, to magnify the Lord. Are we practicing habits that allow us to do that? Or are we practicing the habits that get in the way?

Are we magnifying God by holding on to this grudge? By watching every minute of that steamy streaming series? By joining in the exasperated watercooler discussion about the new boss? By harshly confronting someone on social media, on the sidelines of a sporting contest, or in the school board meeting?

We *know* the answers to those questions. And we know what happens when we instead choose to forgive, to step away from gossip, to try to honor God's ways in public and private.

It's not easy to discipline ourselves to magnify the Lord, but that is part of doing the work. And when we do, the Bible says that we will be *nâhar*: we will be radiant, "lightened." In other words, that is when we will find hope.

Reflection

What are three ways that you are trying to magnify God in your life these days? Thank God for His grace to maintain those. What are three main ways you might *not* be magnifying Him? What can you do to work on those so that you help others—and yourself—see Him more clearly?

"What multiplies is only up to us. Whether it is kindness that multiplies; or unkindness. Whether it is goodwill that multiplies; or bad intentions. Whether it is love that multiplies; or fear. . . . What you magnify upon will in fact become your reality."

—C. JoyBell C.

Day 31

Your word is a lamp to my feet and a light to my path.

—Psalm 119:105, ESV

One Step at a Time

Even with the hope of heaven, it can be hard to face something big. It feels as if we are standing on the rim of the Grand Canyon at midnight, being asked to make it to the other side—and we have no idea how to get there.

Luke was in middle school when we discovered his epilepsy. As I mentioned earlier, it impacted his brain, creating severe processing issues. He spent years learning to read and think all over again. Would he be able to graduate, make friends, or live an independent life? It was a confusing, traumatic time.

We needed guidance so badly, and I eventually saw some embedded in the imagery of this promise: "Your word is a lamp to my feet and a light to my path."

I wanted to see across the Grand Canyon; to see the outcome and how to get there. And yet, an oil lamp illuminates just one or two steps at a time. Which is usually the way God works, right? Do we *ever* see the end at the beginning? No. Our Father wants us to stay close and rely on Him. So He illuminates one step. We take that step, then wait and watch. We must trust that God will guide, that

He will show the next step. And the next.

Our family was anxious for solutions, but God gave us steps. We tried this therapy. Then that one. This testing, that specialist. Luke worked so very hard, and some efforts bombed. There were a lot of tears, as Luke felt despair and we felt hopeless. We were stumbling around in the dark on the canyon floor. It was only later that we realized that some disappointments led to essential steps we wouldn't have considered otherwise.

As the years went by, we realized we were much further down the path than we would have thought possible. It can still feel hard. Big. But whenever we quail at the path ahead, we look at the path behind. We remind ourselves of just how purposefully God has led us. Because God has done so much more than just build our son's ability to learn. He has been building his faith—and ours. That's what happens when you follow each step.

To read more about Luke's story, search for the blog titled "An Amazing Milestone in Our Family—And For Our Son" at Shaunti.com.

Reflection

What feels big to you right now? What small faithful step do you need to take today? What would help you build your trust as you wait to be shown the next step?

*And I said to [him]:
"Give me a light that I may
tread safely into the unknown."
And he replied: "Go out into
the darkness and put your hand
into the Hand of God. That
shall be to you better than light
and safer than a known way."*

—Minnie Louise Haskins, *"The Gate of the Year"*

Day 32

God sent forth his Son . . . so that we might receive adoption as sons. . . . So you are no longer a slave, but a son, and if a son, then an heir through God.

—Galatians 4:4-5, 7, ESV

We Are Chosen and Forever His

At a recent staff meeting, as we introduced two new team members, I was amazed to realize that four of the eight women on my core team were adoptive parents. Some had adopted internationally, some domestically through foster care; some families had biological children, some didn't.

No two adoption stories are alike, but each child is loved and purposely chosen by their adoptive parents. And each has been given the same emotional, physical, and legal privileges as one born into that family. Yet a common theme for many adoptive families is that an adopted child wonders if they are truly, deeply *loved* as much as another child.

We wonder the same thing, right? In Paul's letter we are told repeatedly that we have been "adopted" into the family of God. But there are days when that feels like more of a sideways snub than a blessing. We wonder if we are "less than." We don't always *feel* loved, and we wonder if our heavenly Father is merely tolerating us. Or worse, waiting to dump some new difficulty on us.

Once we understand what adoption meant to the first-century reader, we should never wonder that again. Paul was writing to Gentile believers who lived under Roman law, which was in direct contrast to Jewish law. Jewish law had no legal adoptions, so extended family cared for orphaned children without them becoming legal heirs. By contrast, legal adoption was common in Roman culture—and often occurred with adults! These were usually slaves who had grown up in and were beloved members of the family. The adopted son or daughter started with *no* rights but was granted the full rights and privileges of heirship. Just as important, adoption was irrevocable and legally *stronger* than a blood tie. Biological children could be disowned; adopted children could not. They were forever part of the family.

So when Paul's Gentile readers read that followers of Christ have been "adopted" into God's family, they would have been astonished at the promise. Such an act was driven by active *pursuit* of the adopted person. It was legal. And it was forever. Paul says that adopting us "is what [God] wanted to do, and it gave him great pleasure" (Ephesians 1:5, NLT). Let us never wonder again if we are "less than," and instead remind ourselves that we are *chosen* and forever loved by our heavenly Father.

Reflection

Do you ever feel insecure in God's love—for example, wondering if He might be waiting in the wings to dump some new difficulty on you? How might it change your view to understand the Roman view of adoption? Write a prayer to God thanking Him for choosing you and telling Him that you accept His great love for you.

"I believed that there was a God because I was told it by my grandmother and later by other adults. But when I found . . . that I was a child of God, when I understood that, when I comprehended that, when I internalized that, ingested that, I became courageous."

—Maya Angelou

Day 33

What is more, I consider everything a loss because of the surpassing worth of knowing Christ Jesus my Lord, for whose sake I have lost all things. I consider them garbage, that I may gain Christ.

—Philippians 3:8

Long for Him

As I write these words, I'm thirsty. Thankfully, I'm in a beautiful resort, a few hours away from speaking at a women's retreat, and there's a vending machine right outside my room. Aaah . . . instant satisfaction. Beyond drinks and snacks, there are even more expensive vending machines today that offer electronic equipment, makeup, clothing . . . even cars! We love a machine that gives us exactly what we want, when we want it, don't we?

And sometimes we do that with God. We want something *from* Him. We pray, but mostly because we are looking for answers. Or we long for Jesus because we need comfort and are promised an eternal future, free from pain, tears, disappointment, and heartache. And yes, that *should* be appealing. But God is not our "feel good" vending machine. We're not meant to be in relationship with Him merely for the answers to prayer (only the positive ones, please!), the blessings, the miracles, and the promise of heaven. We're meant to be in relationship with Him for the sake of being in relationship with Him.

Before he was the apostle Paul, Saul had every possible religious blessing available. He had the best bloodline and knew all the right people. He was the world's biggest rule-follower and had all the punches on his pedigree card. But then something happened: he met Jesus. On the road to Damascus, everything he longed for changed. Paul was no longer satisfied with his list of accomplishments. His hunger and thirst could never be sated by the accolades—much less by a quick fix. Once he knew Jesus, all he had originally counted as a big deal was so unimportant it was worth throwing away.

Jesus doesn't exist for our refreshment or consumption. He is the Son of God! He existed before all things. He left heaven *for us,* died to redeem us, and wants a personal relationship with us. When we long for Jesus Himself rather than the good things He gives us, or a quick fix of relief or comfort, we will gain the hope found only in relationship with Him. In this world, we will always have the vending-machine temptation. And we must fight it, for *He* is our ultimate comfort and relief.

Reflection

How have you treated Jesus like a vending machine? What feelings do you experience when you want a quick fix from Him—and what happens when you don't get what you want? What one thing might you do differently to cultivate your *relationship* with Jesus and establish a different pattern that isn't just looking for a quick fix?

"God doesn't comfort us to make us comfortable, but to make us comforters."

—Billy Graham

Day 34

Don't have anything to do with foolish and stupid arguments, because you know they produce quarrels. And the Lord's servant must not be quarrelsome but must be kind to everyone [and] not resentful.

—2 Timothy 2:23-24

Avoiding the Arguments

A few months into the COVID–19 pandemic, a group of friends was debating how church leaders wanted to handle certain things. Suddenly, someone rolled their eyes and blurted out that a particular decision was "stupid."

After an awkward pause, the discussion continued—with an edgier tone. The words were a bit harsher; the body language chillier. Within weeks, the continuing arguments had resulted in everything from minor splinters of friendships to major fractures in support for the pastors. The arguments ended up impacting the witness of the church.

How many of us have seen that dynamic played out over and over again, in person or online, about *any* controversy in our culture? And how many of us have been tempted to jump in? Sharing our perspective requires one click—and there are so many important, debatable issues that can capture our hearts and minds.

Yet God tells us to avoid being captured. Instead of keeping a keen eye on the fights on social media or in the news, He asks us to avoid them—even grieve them. Instead of chiming in, we are called to run the other direction, especially when the person on the other side is a brother or sister in Christ.

Why? Because in God's economy, no issue is worth wrecking our kindness and our witness to others. Yes, there are some essential issues out there, just as there were in the first century. Timothy was fighting deep heresy, for example, with eternal souls at stake. And yet Paul said to "keep reminding God's people" that quarreling "only ruins those who listen" (2 Timothy 2:14).

There's nothing wrong with passionate beliefs. But ask yourself when you feel most filled with hope—when you enter into the arguments of the day or when you determine not to? In our heated exchanges, our hearts are often trapped by disagreements about issues rather than caring for the people behind the issues. When that happens, we may not focus on what Jesus wants our hearts to be set on—or on the *process* of how He wants us to engage with others.

And when we bicker within the church, a watching world that desperately needs Jesus is not seeing Him. They're seeing unkindness and a focus on the things of this world instead of the One who has overcome the world.

Let's resolve to be people of hope instead of people who quarrel, knowing which one will draw others to Jesus.

Reflection

Do you ever find yourself getting caught up in debates or arguments over cultural or personal issues? (Politics, education, social issues, family dynamics, etc.?) If so, how do they impact your spirit, mood, or relationships? Identify three ways you can prevent or avoid quarrels—especially with fellow believers—in order to be a picture of hope in a struggling world.

*"Quarrels end,
but words
once spoken
never die."*

—African Proverb

Day 35

"For my thoughts are not your thoughts, neither are your ways my ways," declares the LORD. "As the heavens are higher than the earth, so are my ways higher than your ways and my thoughts than your thoughts."

—Isaiah 55:8–9

We May Not Know

I have a picture of myself staring out at the Pacific Ocean on a gray, sad day. The photographer had no idea that I was coming to terms with this Scripture, but when she sent me the picture she had superimposed this verse across the sky.

Naomi Duncan helped me start my ministry in 2004. She was my speaking agent and one of my closest confidants—a sister and friend. Naomi was the mom of two teenagers and the wife of a pastor. They planted a church near Portland, where very few attend church, and I'm convinced God picked them for that area partly because Naomi drew everyone to Jesus through her sweet and snappy spirit. (Think, someone wise and kind who also makes you snort with laughter.)

When Naomi had routine surgery in 2020 at a small local hospital, our team wasn't worried. But there were complications. We hoped the small hospital would send her to a big hospital in Portland. They sent her home instead. I soon got a terrible call—Naomi had collapsed from a pulmonary embolism, fought for hours, and passed away.

We were in shock. How could this healthy woman in her 40s, with two children, who loved her husband, who adored her church, who had so many people relying on her strength, who had such a ministry . . . be gone? It didn't make sense.

You may have stories like that too. The common denominator of all grief and suffering is bewilderment, right? We don't understand. We want to try to figure it out. We want to know why God allowed it. We want to use our minds to make sense of something that seems completely nonsensical.

God has a purpose, even in suffering. But as I stared out at that turbulent ocean following my friend's funeral, I had to acknowledge that He will not always show us what it is. We can only recognize that we are under the care of a great big God who put the stars into motion and lovingly created every cell in our bodies. That He spoke into being every person, mountain, and wave we see around us, and He can be trusted with everything we don't see behind the veil of heaven.

For all of us, trying to "figure it out" leads only to bewilderment. We must say, "Your ways are higher" before we can find real hope.

Reflection

Have you had any hard experiences in which you tried to "figure it out" and make sense of something that didn't make sense? Did that help, and bring peace and understanding, or not so much? What can you lay down at His feet today, and how might that change things now?

"The best proof of love is trust."

—Dr. Joyce Brothers

Day 36

Whatever you do, work at it with all your heart,
as working for the Lord,
not for human masters.

—Colossians 3:23

The Power of the Small Things

Years ago, I was struck by a comment from a movie reviewer who had never read the *Lord of the Rings* books but was reviewing the movies. In the final review of *The Return of the King,* this reviewer said (and I'm paraphrasing here), "It is an astounding thing to get to the end of a long, three-movie story and realize that the hero isn't who you thought it was all along."

The story centers on Frodo, who goes on a harrowing journey carrying the evil One Ring to the place where he can destroy it and save Middle Earth. Traveling with him is Sam, his faithful and unassuming sidekick and encourager. Sam can't do the big task of carrying the Ring, so he does the little ones. But in the end, all hope looks lost. Frodo and Sam haven't had water in days and have collapsed. Sam suddenly pushes to his feet, crying, "I can't carry it for you, but I can carry *you*!" He puts Frodo on his back and struggles the final steps up the mountain.

I find myself in tears at that scene. It so profoundly illustrates the power of being faithful in the little things.

I am convinced that when we get to heaven, we will see that the true heroes of faith are those who quietly live a faithful life (Matthew 6:6). The praying grandmother who spends hours on her knees; the mom who constantly drives her special-needs child to therapy; the person who checks in on a depressed friend; the retiree who cooks meals at the local shelter. They do these things without recognition, often never knowing the impacts of their actions . . . but they are carrying others.

Shortly after learning I had breast cancer, I received a call from a woman I had met only once before. She told me that for several months *before* my diagnosis, she had sensed God saying, "Pray for Shaunti every Friday." She had no idea why until then. Her faithfulness deeply bolstered my hope when I needed it most.

We need to remind ourselves that as we go about "minor" tasks—praying for someone, running an errand for a neighbor, cooking meals for our family—this is the work of heaven, if we do it for Him. This is building a life that is filled with hope and sharing that hope with others. God uses our ordinary, faithful actions for extraordinary impact.

Reflection

What are the works of heaven that no one will see that you have been called to faithfully do? List several of those things here and ponder: What might God do through you in those small things that could end up having a big impact? Commit those hopes to Him.

"But the effect of [Dorothea's] being on those around her was incalculably diffusive: for the growing good of the world is partly dependent on unhistoric acts; and that things are not so ill with you and me as they might have been, is half owing to the number who lived faithfully a hidden life, and rest in unvisited tombs."

—George Eliot, MIDDLEMARCH

Day 37

Not that we are adequate in ourselves to consider anything as coming from ourselves, but our adequacy is from God.

—2 Corinthians 3:5, NASB 1995

We Can't Hope in Ourselves

Twenty years ago, our friends adopted a twelve-year-old from Russia. "Nadia" had lived on the streets, so her adoptive parents poured into her all the warmth and love she needed. But sadly, Nadia never truly, down deep, *believed* in their love. Something inside her said, *I will not let myself hope that these people actually love me.* She didn't trust. She believed her only hope was handling things herself.

So Nadia left home when she turned 18. Since then, her family has only periodically known of her whereabouts. Texts and calls are rare.

Nadia's story is so sad . . . but should also sound familiar. Don't we, to one degree or another, exhibit similar behavior toward God? We don't *let* ourselves hope in Him, even when we need Him.

The first example of this occurs immediately after sin enters the world. Adam and Eve realize they are naked, but instead of asking God for clothing, they attempt to sew fig leaves together as coverings. Their default reaction is the same as ours—self-rescue instead of allowing ourselves to believe God will rescue us.

We make ourselves crazy trying to solve a financial problem, get in good with the boss so we don't lose the promotion, or convince the school to address a bully instead of simply doing what we can do (like reporting it and setting boundaries), and then allowing God to do what only He can do.

Why? Simple: We don't trust Him! Down deep, we don't fully believe in God's goodness and His love for us. The most foundational reason Eve ate the forbidden fruit was her suspicion that God was purposefully withholding something good from her.

Our efforts to hope in ourselves never work in the end. Things go wrong and we get even more dejected. But there's good news! When we finally recognize that we can't fully hope in ourselves—that we need God to solve the financial or bullying problem, or when we trust that the promotion will come *if* that is God's best plan for us—that's when we finally find *real* hope.

Nadia's parents haven't given up on her. They still pursue her and long to see her. Their arms are always open. Thankfully, God is the same way. He didn't roll His eyes at Adam and Eve's futile efforts to cover themselves; He gave them clothes. God doesn't lose patience even when we go our own way. We can trust and hope in this loving Father whose arms remain open.

Reflection

Is there anything you are struggling with, something you are trying to control (perhaps by running away from it) and in which you need to trust God? What might the scary step of doing what you can do and then truly trusting God with your concern actually look like?

"Following Christ is a wild adventure full of risk, frustration, excitement, and setbacks. It is not an evening stroll in a planned community along a well-manicured path."

—Larry Crabb

Day 38

He comforts us in all our troubles so that we can comfort others. When they are troubled, we will be able to give them the same comfort God has given us.

—2 Corinthians 1:4, NLT

Custom-Fit Grace

Why is it that comparing our life with others is such a trap for our heart? Well, a main reason we get jealous or downcast is that we compare our valleys to someone else's peaks. But the reality is, everyone has both. And we might be surprised if we saw the full scope of what others carry. We might even begin to have gratitude instead of envy.

My husband Jeff has a group of fifteen friends from law school who get together each year. Some of these men have become incredibly influential or wealthy. Some hold important leadership positions. Others try not to be envious. But one late night over cards, they talked about it. And as they opened up about their lives, they realized that each of them has a mix of beautiful blessings and real hardships.

This person had an enviable job but a spouse who had serious cancer. This guy had properties all over the world but very painful problems with his kids. This person had a great marriage but significant financial hardship.

Someone asked, "If we were to each shove the 'package' of our lives to the center of this table so we could trade with someone else—would you pick up someone else's package?" They all realized they would probably take back their own.

Friends, *we have been given the grace for what God allows in our lives.* We may not immediately see it that way because it feels hard. But God's grace and comfort for our particular hardship is there. It is easy to think, *I would trade struggling to make ends meet for being wealthy but struggling with my kids.* But if such a trade were somehow possible, we would probably discover that we actually wouldn't!

Once we see God's unique comfort for us, we see other things as well: Gratitude for the gifts we have been given. And even a purpose in the hardships, as we have special ability to speak into the lives of others who are struggling in similar ways.

Are there parts of your life you keep trying to push to the center of the table? Pick those back up in trust. Think through the gifts you have and thank God for them. Then ask Him to show you how He's given you grace for the whole package—and how He wants to use you to extend that grace to others.

Reflection

What parts of your life do you compare to others and wish were different? What parts of your life do you love and wouldn't trade for anything? Thank God for the whole package, and ask Him to show you how He has given you grace for the hard things—and how you can comfort others in those areas.

"Jesus lost all his glory so that we could be clothed in it. . . . He was bound, nailed, so that we could be free. . . . And Jesus took away the only kind of suffering that can really destroy you: that is being cast away from God. [So] now all suffering that comes into your life will only make you great. A lump of coal under pressure becomes a diamond."

—Tim Keller

Day 39

You are not your own; you were bought at a price.

—1 Corinthians 6:19-20

Your Purchase Price Proves Your Worth

Recently I was moved by a scene in a novel, a fictionalized version of the ultimate True Story. Brutal terrorists have taken many hostages and are killing them one at a time. An important woman is about to be killed, and rescue forces are still too far away. So a heroic soldier who is the terrorists' particular enemy trades himself for that hostage, buying time for the rescue forces to save everyone else as well—even though, in the end, they wouldn't be in time to save him.

Why did he sacrifice himself? Because she was the woman he loved. Until then, she wasn't sure of that fact. But whatever worries she may have had about his care for her, or doubts about whether she was worthy of his love, were wiped away. Buying her life with his demonstrated, more than anything could have, what she was worth to him.

In the quiet of our hearts, we can question whether we are valuable or special. We wonder things like, *Does my husband* really *love me?* Or *Would my friends still like me if they saw the "real me"?* These doubts point to the most secret question of all: *Am I worthy of being loved? Even by God?*

Those doubts drain the life out of us. They breed insecurity. Fear. We try to put on a good front and hide our flaws. We seek a sense of worth in our romantic relationship *(I must be lovable if* he *loves me!*) or our friendships. But it doesn't work. We are still insecure. So we think our children or our job can give us worth. But then our kids misbehave or the job doesn't work out, and we think we look bad. We feel even worse.

We'll never find true security until we grasp with utter certainty the truth that our value comes solely from *God's* assessment of our worth.

You can tell how much a person values something based on how much they will spend to purchase it. And our purchase price was the life of Jesus, who gave Himself up so we might live. How infinitely precious we are! It should take our breath away. So when we feel the walls of insecurity closing in, or the accusations of the enemy that we are not loved and lovable, we must lift our heads and remind ourselves that we are worth the ultimate price.

Reflection

Put your name in the blank and read this out loud:

Jesus finds me, ______________, worthy of loving enough to die for. I am precious, honored in His sight, and loved beyond measure (Isaiah 43:4). I am chosen (Isaiah 44:1) by my Redeemer, who formed me in my mother's womb (Isaiah 44:24). My hope is an anchor for my soul, firm and secure in the work of Jesus on my behalf (Hebrews 6:19). He loves me and always will. His love cannot and will not change. I am dearly loved.

How does it change your mindset to realize that Jesus loves you enough to *die* for you? What should you do differently based on that realization?

"Love is when a man
wipes your tears,
even after you left
Him hanging on the
cross for your sins."

—Author Unknown

Day 40

Love is patient, love is kind and is not jealous; love does not brag and is not arrogant, does not act unbecomingly; it does not seek its own, is not provoked, does not take into account a wrong suffered, does not rejoice in unrighteousness, but rejoices with the truth; bears all things, believes all things, hopes all things, endures all things.

—1 Corinthians 13:4-7, NASB1995

Is Our Love Patient?

Who hasn't heard "Love is patient, love is kind . . ." read in a marriage ceremony? "Love bears all things, believes all things, hopes all things, endures all things." Most of us can probably recite 1 Corinthians 13 by heart along with the pastor or officiant. We use it as a sweet sentiment on decorative pillows, framed artwork, and desk plaques.

I suspect that if we really understood what that famous passage is saying, we would see it entirely differently at a wedding. And we would only display it on artwork as a much-needed reminder and challenge.

Why? Because it isn't a sweet sentiment. It's actually a rebuke from Paul to the Christians in the city of Corinth. In his letter, Paul discusses some drama happening in the church, outlines some rules for Christian living, and then essentially says, "But most importantly, you guys are not doing a great job of being people of love. So let me describe for you what love actually is, so you can see what we, the followers of Jesus, should look like."

Now let's read 1 Corinthians 13 again—and be honest with ourselves. Am I patient with that frustrating colleague? Am I kind to that person who is mean to me? Am I not boastful when I drop a humble brag about how much I enjoyed that trip for the top customer service reps? Am I keeping a record of wrongs when my boyfriend yet again does that thing that drives me nuts?

We all need God's power to live up to God's high calling of love. And this deeply matters for hope. ("Love hopes all things . . .") You know that child, friend, or family member you have been trying to help, who keeps making self-destructive choices? Don't give up on them. Fix your eyes on God's power to transform, and keep loving them. You know how your spouse has been struggling for years with his job? Love means not losing hope to support him. You know how you sometimes feel hopeless yourself? Be kind and loving to yourself, and don't ever give up.

Being a follower of Jesus means holding on to the hope that comes through the power of God and loving people no matter what. Let us put "Love hopes all things" on our pillows and artwork, and accept that high calling—that challenge—as followers of Christ.

Reflection

In what part of your life do you find yourself struggling with hope today? Is it worry for a friend's marriage? Your child's future? Your own emotional health? What would it look like to be (or continue to be) loving in that situation, and how would that build your hope?

"You never so touch the ocean of God's love as when you forgive and love your enemies."

—Corrie ten Boom

Day 41

Therefore, go and make disciples of all the nations. . . . Teach these new disciples to obey all the commands I have given you.

—Matthew 28:19-20, NLT

As You Are Already Going

The idiom "bloom where you are planted" dates back centuries. We see it as encouraging us to find joy no matter our circumstances—which it does. But in a way, it also reflects Christ's final instructions before His ascension. Known as the "Great Commission," in Matthew 28 Jesus tells His followers to go out into the world and make disciples.

When I was new in my faith, in my midtwenties, I always found that idea a bit intimidating. Certainly not a cause for hope. Why? Because I thought it meant, essentially, "Stop what you are doing and get out there! Do something new and different to spread the gospel." Was I supposed to leave the job I loved on Capitol Hill and move overseas to be a missionary? I had just been admitted to Harvard for grad school—did following the Great Commission mean working for a church or evangelism ministry instead?

While some of us are indeed called to start a brand-new life of "professional ministry," that is not the language here. The Greek word used for "go" in this passage is *poreuō*, which means "to continue on one's journey." Jesus is saying, "In the ways you are already going, make disciples."

In other words: *Bloom where you are already planted, and help others follow Me.*

You are called to love others and make disciples in your daily sphere of influence. You are already a teacher, a mom, a dentist, a caregiver, a marketing executive. How can you love others in the name of Jesus and help them follow Him? Perhaps you can offer to pray for your fellow teacher who is having a really bad and discouraging day. Perhaps on a playdate you share coffee with the other mom and encourage her in her marriage, using Biblical truths that have helped your own relationship. Maybe your colleague mentions that they used to go to church as a child, and you invite them to join you on Sunday.

You don't need to "get out there"; you are already out there! So because you love Jesus, keep looking for ways to love and serve those with whom you come into contact. Because you love Jesus, keep looking to share the Good News. He will provide the opportunities for you to spread hope to everyone around you.

Reflection

Make a list of the ways that you could fulfill the command to "go and make disciples" in your daily life. Ask God to show you four or five people you could share with, encourage, or help in their walk with Jesus.

"The more we know and love Jesus, the more we will be fearless in talking about Him. . . .This is the most significant news anyone can ever hear, let us not be afraid to spread this Good News."

—Father Sean Magaldi

Day 42

Do not be anxious about anything, but in every situation, by prayer and petition, with thanksgiving, present your requests to God. And the peace of God, which transcends all understanding, will guard your hearts and your minds in Christ Jesus.

—Philippians 4:6-7

Pray More, Worry Less

Jasmine had spent another night worrying and planning for the consequences of her husband's job transfer—moving to a different state, new schools for the kids, being far from family and friends. The next morning, she had breakfast with some girlfriends and shared her concerns and prayer requests.

Later, as they browsed the shop next to the restaurant, Jasmine noticed a plaque that said, "Pray more, worry less." She paused, then moved on. But those four words stayed in her mind all day. Pray more, worry less. That evening, after talking with her husband and her mother about her schooling concerns, and after about a thousand more moving-related thoughts, plans, and emails, that phrase was still in her mind.

Suddenly, Jasmine realized why. For days, she had been thinking about the move. She had been talking to people about the move. She had been worrying about the move. But she hadn't actually been praying about the move. All her activity had masked the fact that she hadn't actually sat down with the Lord and talked to *Him.*

If we're honest with ourselves, a lot of us could say the same. Thinking and planning and talking things over with people can be helpful and healthy, but none of that substitutes for going to our heavenly Father and handing Him our concerns.

The problem is, it can be easier to hand our problems to a friend. It can be easier to create one more planning document, send one more school email, or discuss it one more time with our spouse. By contrast, we must *choose* to pray about our worries, thank God that He is in control, and trust Him to work.

That trust is where hope lives. Because all the talking, planning, and emailing in the world won't necessarily help us understand or create the best outcome for whatever worries us. But when we pray, we are talking things over with the only One who *does* know the best outcome—and can deliver it! That brings real comfort. Real hope.

What is your area of worry? Where are you tempted to buzz around in planning and thinking and seeking guidance—of everyone except your heavenly Father? Take some time to sit with Him instead, thank Him for His work, and breathe in His comfort and peace.

Reflection

What concerns are you thinking and talking about lately? Schedule time for the next days or weeks ahead (literally put those times on your calendar) to sit and talk things over with the Lord. Journal what comes of those times with Him.

"No one can worry and pray at the same time."

—Max Lucado

Day 43

I have seen you in the sanctuary and
beheld your power and your glory.
. . . I cling to you; your right hand upholds me.

–Psalms 63:2, 8

Seeing the Bigger Picture

A dear friend and her husband were facing a desperate situation with their family, fighting against a court influenced by lies that was considering taking their children away. Many people prayed for a just outcome. But the lies prevailed and my friends lost their children, with no sense of when they would return or even when they could contact them. The family was devastated.

We cried the words of Psalm 73:1-3—*Why do the wicked prosper?* How could God allow this to happen?

But God's perspective is so much larger than our limited view. As the tears flowed that day, a memory came to mind. I was twenty-one years old, backpacking across Europe with a friend. We arrived in Rome to see St. Peter's Basilica, one of the largest churches in the world. We were hot and sweaty, at odds with each other, and worried about a major travel problem. But as we stepped into the huge church, all of that fell away. We were silenced by the scope and the majesty surrounding us.

We—and all of our problems—suddenly felt so small.

A tour guide pointed toward the ceiling soaring above us and the Latin characters carved high on the wall. "How tall do you think those carvings are?" They looked pretty large—maybe two or even three feet tall. He said, "They're *nine* feet tall." We couldn't wrap our minds around it. The scale was so enormous, and our perspective so small, that we couldn't accurately perceive it.

That's just a taste of what the psalmist means when he says, "I have seen you in the sanctuary and beheld your power and your glory." God's sheer majesty is beyond our comprehension. And He is in control. When He allows things to happen that we don't understand, we might initially cry, *God, You're not doing anything!* But we must shift our perspective. Our problems may be big, but they are small compared to God's power, His love for us, and His larger purposes in the world.

Over the course of six long months of no contact with their children, my friends found that against all odds their devastation was replaced by hope. It was still hard. But they couldn't stay hopeless as they sat in the sanctuary, constantly reminding themselves that an infinitely majestic God was in control.

Reflection

Have you ever questioned why God would allow something bad to happen to someone who tries to follow Him well? Or allow something good to happen to a wicked person? How might "entering the sanctuary" provide the perspective you need?

"I'm not worshipping
God because today
is good. I'm worshipping
God because
God is good
—even today."

—Mark Hall

Day 44

Peter turned and saw that the disciple whom Jesus loved was following them. . . . When Peter saw him, he asked, "Lord, what about him?" Jesus answered, "If I want him to remain alive until I return, what is that to you? You must follow me."

—John 21:20-22

What about Them?

More times than I'd like to admit, I notice other people's lives. Candidly, it's usually something like, *Why doesn't she struggle with her weight like I do?* Or, *Oh wow.* <Big sigh> *I wish we could afford that kitchen remodel.*

Social media provides limitless opportunities to compare ourselves with others. You see a friend's family photo taken on a sunset beach with matching—but not too matching—clothes, everyone smiling brightly. Yet you feel like you're lucky to get a family picture at all, much less one with everyone's eyes open, looking at the camera, and holding off squabbling for a few blessed minutes.

It is so easy to ask, "Why them and not me?" Or, conversely, "Why are these bad things happening to just me?" Those questions drain hope and joy out of us because they make us believe we have so many struggles and others (seemingly) do not. Is God playing favorites?

God graciously answers our question, but we might not like what He says because the answer is also the antidote to the temptation to compare: Ultimately, their stories are none of our business.

In C. S. Lewis's book *The Horse and His Boy*, the main character asks Aslan, the Jesus figure, about another person's fate. Aslan replies, "Child . . . I am telling you your story, not hers. No one is told any story but their own." Jesus said much the same thing. He had just given Peter a hint of how Peter would die, when Peter looks at John and asks, "what about him?" Jesus replies, "what is that to you? You must follow me."

This is crucial: God wants us to follow Him and focus on our own story, not simply to avoid being nosy but in order to find His blessing! Moments before Peter asked that question, Jesus had been sharing what should have been deep reassurances that He cared for Peter, despite those three denials when Jesus was arrested. Yet Peter gets focused on wondering, *What about this other guy's life?* In the moment (hopefully until Jesus snapped him out of it!) Peter seems to have entirely missed the astounding, relentless love Jesus was offering him. All because Peter took his eyes off Jesus and put them on another person.

Friends, let's fight that tendency. Let's keep our eyes squarely on the One who has an astounding, relentless love for *us*. Because that is where we will find our hope.

Reflection

What can you do to make comparison less of a challenge? (For example, taking a break from social media, thanking God for His blessing on the lives of others, and so on.) Also, what are five blessings of the life you have been given that you can be thankful for today?

"If you try to be someone else, you rob God of who He is trying to make YOU to be."

—Miles McPherson

Day 45

For God has not given us a spirit of fear,
but of power and of love and of a sound mind.

—2 Timothy 1:7, NKJV

Don't Let Fear Cast Out Love

Why was the first-century church so filled with hope? Why were *so many* getting saved, with this brand-new faith spreading across the earth at unimaginable speed? Early Christians had *none* of what we think is important for the protection and thriving of our faith today. They had no political power, no authority in government, no religious liberties. It was actually the opposite.

In some regions the Christian minority had no power, but were at least left alone in a pluralistic society. Or they were treated like many are treated today—with a shrug ("Whatever does it for you, man") or a roll of the eyes. But in many regions, over many years, followers of the Way were not just "not in power," they were ruthlessly persecuted by the governing system of the day.

And yet, the gospel exploded. Perhaps not *in spite of* the persecution but *because* of it. When Christians were herded to the lions, onlookers noted that "they died well." And in the face of normal daily tribulations, society saw an unexplainable hope in these followers of the Way.

Why? Because their message was not based on having the right words, or the ability to freely share those words, but on the pure love of Jesus.

Today, as followers of Jesus become a smaller and smaller minority in our culture, we can have a spirit of fear that tells us, "we need to fight to keep our religious liberties!" or "if this particular cultural movement takes hold, we will lose this country!" And of course there are many vitally important things that we *should* work and pray for. But let us never forget that our ultimate citizenship is not in this country but in heaven. Let us never forget that our ultimate calling is not to protect ourselves or even others (as good as that is) but to *love*. To love no matter what.

To even love those who are persecuting us. I think I've read that somewhere. . . .

It is hard to be loving when we are defensive. And we are defensive when we are afraid of loss.

What if, like the first-century Christians, we eventually hold no authority, no power, and lose all our liberties? Where will our hope be? Will we despair? Or will our hope be untouched because it has nothing to do with power or rights? Let us always rest in—and show—only the hope and love of Jesus.

Reflection

When you think about what is happening in culture, do you ever find yourself in the grip of fear rather than faith? If so, write down three things that you are afraid of happening or losing (e.g., "I'm afraid Christians will no longer be allowed to openly share what we believe"). Then, write down how the first-century church might have responded to each problem. Does that give you any ideas for how *you* might respond today?

"We do not fear the loss of God's favor, for either we have it [or] not. We cannot lose it. What we fear is the loss of our idols."

—R. C. Sproul, Jr.

Day 46

But they who wait for the LORD shall renew their strength; they shall mount up with wings like eagles; they shall run and not be weary; they shall walk and not faint.

—Isaiah 40:31, ESV

Soaring toward the Storm

Have you ever walked down the sidewalk looking at your phone and nearly bumped into someone? Me neither (ahem).

Our body will drift where our gaze is fixed—and it works the same way with hope. As we have already discovered, we gain strength to endure as we lift our eyes from our circumstances and gaze on our heavenly Father instead. But think about it: that also means we are facing *toward* our circumstances instead of away from them.

Most of us try to run from trouble. We avoid having that difficult conversation with a wayward friend to avoid a conflict. We avert our gaze from certain problems at the office because we don't want to "get involved." Or we try to jolly our daughter out of her funk that she didn't make the volleyball team. We try to be happier and more hopeful by *avoiding* difficulty. Yet those very difficulties are what perpetually pull us closer to God. Our fearful efforts to avoid trouble actually sabotage our ability to find the encouragement we need!

Have you ever watched massive birds soaring in the air? Scientists discovered that eagles in flight often head into, rather than away from, a storm. Eagles use the atmospheric pressure of the storm to soar, and they are carried above the clouds to a view they could never have had otherwise.

We can do the same. This doesn't mean we "go looking for trouble," of course. But when we see storms coming, we can realize the pressure doesn't have to be a bad thing if we handle it in trust. Isaiah tells us, "They who wait for the Lord shall renew their strength; they shall mount up with wings like eagles." The word *wait* is also translated "hope" or "expect." So as we soar toward those stormy circumstances—as we work through the difficult conversation with the friend and wait to see how God will use it—we *expect* that He will give us the strength we need.

And just as we watch the eagles navigating turbulence, there are people watching us. So as we enter into our daughter's sadness about volleyball, as she sees that her heartbreak matters, we gain the credibility to say, "Honey, trust that God has something better." Then we can watch, together, as God opens up an opportunity she never would have had otherwise, carrying her—and us—above the clouds.

Reflection

Is there a potential trouble in sight? Something heavy on your heart that you have been trying to avoid? How might that change as you head towards the storm looking to God for strength and persepctive?

"God says I am making all things new. He doesn't say I am making all new things. He is in the business of restoring what is broken."

—Andrew Peterson

Day 47

Do your best to present yourself to God
as one approved, a worker who does
not need to be ashamed and who
correctly handles the word of truth.

—2 Timothy 2:15

Aim for Only One Approval

Do you ever mentally review a tricky social or work event? Perhaps you think things like, *She didn't even say hello* or *I could have said that so much better* (complete with endless ideas of what you *should* have said) or *They acted really strange; I wonder if they are angry with me.* For me, doubts about whether others are pleased with me can fly around like a flurry of startled birds in my mind.

Caring about social interactions is perfectly fine. And we are instructed to try to "live at peace with everyone" (Romans 12:18). But when *pleasing* others becomes our goal, it can rob us of hope and joy quicker than almost anything else. It leaves us feeling trapped, and we actually *are* trapped if our joy is dependent on the response of someone else!

As children of God, we have an aim and purpose everywhere we go, but it is not to make ourselves look good or to please others at all costs. To the degree we are focused on what others think of us, we are taking an earthly perspective, not a heavenly one. Our verse today exhorts us, "Do your best to present yourself to

God as one approved." *God's* approval should be our aim. And to the extent that we "aim true" in this area, we can enter any social setting with hope and confidence. We now have the only Audience that matters—One who has called us His own. How would this shift in focus change how we interact with people?

Now, to be clear: avoiding a focus on the *approval* of others is not the same as not caring about others' *feelings*. We are called to love one another—and to show it. One of the beautiful dynamics of marriage or friendship is figuring out what blesses others and doing it. But the approval of our spouse, friends, or social media followers can never be the end goal. Because then we will always be one social media troll away from becoming really sad. We will always be conflicted if someone wants us to handle something in a way that runs counter to God's heart.

Just as we learn what matters to those we care about, let's work to seek only what pleases God. Let's work to find ourselves approved by *Him*. And when that security takes up space in our minds and hearts, those startled birds will have no place to circle anymore.

Reflection

Whose approval are you aiming for these days? What would change in your attitude or actions if you aimed for the approval of only One? If you put such a plan into action, what responses (good or bad) might you get from others—and what will help you navigate any negative responses if they come?

"I have learned that the prison of others' approval is actually one built by me, maintained by me, and guarded by me."

—Arthur Brooks

Day 48

Those who plant in tears will harvest with shouts of joy. They weep as they go to plant their seed, but they sing as they return with the harvest.

—**Psalm 126:5-6**, NLT

Grieve What Isn't to Enjoy What Is

As we worked on a marriage book, Jeff and I regularly met with our coauthor, Dr. Michael Sytsma, a renowned Christian sex therapist. (I'll give you one guess what the book was about.) Since this book had to focus on simple factors that mattered to most married couples, rather than specialized issues, we asked Dr. Sytsma: was there any common denominator that would help couples build a great relationship *regardless* of what their issues were?

He smiled. "Actually, every experienced counselor already knows what that common denominator is. In the end, all counseling work is grief work. Something about your spouse isn't what you were hoping for. You have to grieve what isn't and accept what is before you can move forward to enjoy what you have."*

Even beyond marriage, all of us have things that aren't as we hoped. We work so hard to start that business—and it fails. Our son loves video games and has no interest in the family passion of outdoor adventures. Our son-in-law is nice enough, but not the person we would have chosen for our daughter. And our husband loves working with his hands, not in an office; he is probably never going to earn a higher income than he currently earns.

Sadness or disappointment is understandable. But it can also keep us trapped in discontent and discouragement. To find hope, we must first go through something hard: grieving that our desire is never going to happen. Our business has to close. Our child will never really love camping in the way we and his siblings do. Our daughter is never going to have the exact husband we hoped for. And our spouse will never earn enough for us to retire early to the Caymans.

But grieving and letting go of what *isn't* does something remarkable: it allows us to see what *is.* We learned so much from our failed business. Our son is interested in programming and will probably always have a great job. Our son-in-law is really kind and a great father to our grandchildren. And our husband *loves* what he does and never brings work stress home.

Now we have something to not just tolerate, but embrace. Now we have something that builds our hope.

* However, as Dr. Sytsma also makes clear, not all situations are acceptable. Abuse, for example, should never be accepted.

Reflection

Is there a situation in your life that you are disappointed or discouraged about? Is it something you can or should recognize as permanently different from what you wanted, and grieve its loss? How might that free you up to celebrate or enjoy something about the situation instead?

"Forgiveness changes the way we remember."

—Henri Nouwen

Day 49

Guide me in your truth and teach me,
for you are God my Savior,
and my hope is in you all day long.

—**Psalm 25:5**

There's Hope in the Process

Picture two similar Christian moms in this real-life scenario. Each has a daughter in high school, and each is frustrated with a teacher who appears to be very unfair toward them. (For example, by giving more "favored" students the chance to retake tests but refusing to let these girls do so—which might scuttle their straight-A averages and chances of getting into a top college.)

Both students are facing injustice, both moms are very worried and praying about it a lot, and both are trying to address it. Yet their outlook is completely different.

Mom A asked her daughter to advocate for herself with the teacher, and then when that didn't work, she emailed the teacher asking if they could have a phone call. The emails back and forth have not been promising.

Mom B went directly to the school's guidance counselor and academic director and has talked about it with them and other parents. She is seeking anyone who can give her advice, help, and emotional support.

One of these women is intensely stressed and cannot stop thinking about the problem. The other woman is just as concerned, but has a more hopeful outlook and more peace in the waiting. Can you guess which is which? And, even more importantly, *why?*

Mom A is the more peaceful one. She is honoring the *process* that the school has set for dealing with concerns, which is comparable to the biblical process in Matthew 18: The student should go to the teacher first. If that doesn't yield results, *then* the parent can go to the teacher, and only after that (which looks likely to happen) should the parent go to the administration (which she will do next). And don't undermine the teacher by complaining to others.

Mom B views the situation as serious and assumes the usual process is unlikely to work, so she has gone "right to the top" and has stirred up indignation in others. Is it any wonder that she's the one who is also a ball of nerves?

Friends, sometimes "there is a way that appears to be right" to us (Proverbs 14:12), and it can feel justified. But if it is contrary to God's ways, it brings death and a *lack* of hope instead of life. God has given us His ways for good reasons, and one is that a hopeful outlook is often built not by any particular outcome but by following a *process* that honors God in the journey.

Reflection

Think back to a time when you felt that following God's process made no sense. Did you follow it or do your own thing? What was the result? Do you agree that a hopeful outlook is more likely when you follow God's ways, even when things don't end the way you wanted? Write a prayer about this to God.

"I don't have to figure my present circumstances out. I don't have to fill the silence left behind in another person's absence. I don't have to know all the whys and what-ifs. All I have to do is trust. So . . . I make the decision to let God sort it all out."

—Lysa TerKeurst

Day 50

There were also other boats with [Jesus]. A furious squall came up, and the waves broke over the boat, so that it was nearly swamped. . . . [Jesus] said to the waves, "Quiet! Be still!" Then the wind died down and it was completely calm.

—Mark 4:36-37, 39

Other Boats Will Benefit

It was a call no parent ever wants to receive. Celeste and David's college-age son had been killed in a car accident. They were devastated. In that split second their life changed forever.

After the funeral, life continued—as it does—with school for the other kids and work for the adults. Celeste and David had to consciously put one foot in front of the other and learn a new way of living without their son. The days often felt dark, and waves of grief would hit without warning. But in the darkness the whole family clung to the hope they had in Jesus. They knew their son, their brother, who had accepted Christ, was with Him now. And because of that hope, their bone-deep sadness was one they could put into an eternal perspective: the separation was only for a time. They would see him again! It gave them great peace in their grieving.

They also began to see with another type of eternal perspective—that God was using them in the lives of others going through grief and loss. As a general care practitioner, David got many questions from his patients about how his family was coping. As he told the story of how he and Celeste were receiving the peace of Jesus amid this unspeakable loss, his patients listened and took the message to heart. Often they would come back later and tell David that the way he and his family were grieving inspired them to look at their own grief differently. Some began looking into how Jesus could comfort them as well.

Think about this for a moment: when the disciples in the boat were caught in a devastating storm (Mark 4), Jesus commanded the waves to stop—but it wasn't just their own boat that benefitted. There were other boats with them, with other people who were terrified and in need. When Jesus comforted the disciples during their storm, all the others around them received the blessing of peace too.

Celeste and David never would have chosen this type of ministry. But they knew this was a way that what the enemy meant for evil could be turned for good. In our own hard times—times we never would have chosen—we can look to the One who is calming our storm and do the same.

Reflection

How are you dealing with grief these days? It may be the loss of a loved one, of a desired transfer to a different department, or the simple grief of waiting for a desired change that is long in coming. How can you hold on to hope and *share* that hope with others?

"I have learned to kiss the waves that throw me up against the Rock of Ages."

—Author Unknown

Day 51

We can make our own plans, but the LORD gives the right answer. . . .
Commit your actions to the LORD, and your plans will succeed. . . .
We can make our plans, but the LORD determines our steps.

—Proverbs 16:1, 3, 9, NLT

Make Rollable Plans

We all have things we eagerly hope and plan for. We've invested in a new business and want it to go well. We dearly want to get into this graduate school or meet someone on that dating app. We want this certain vacation or that retirement savings balance.

I'm a big one for planning, avoiding as many potential problems as possible, and controlling everything so it happens the way I want.

The problem, of course, is that things often don't happen the way I want. Verses 1 and 9 of Proverbs 16 remind us that we can make our own plans, but in the end the Lord gives us the answer *He* wants. God is the One who determines our steps. We can eagerly hope for something specific, but the results are in God's hands.

But wait! We might think, *What about verse 3?* We like that one a lot better. "Commit your actions to the LORD, and your plans will succeed." Yes, please! We read that as, "OK, God, here's what I want to do. I'm building X or doing Y and committing it to you, so please bless it and bring the answer I want." We determine the plan and invite God to join us.

It should be the other way around.

The Hebrew word for "commit," *gālal*, literally means "to roll upon." In other words, "Roll your actions upon the Lord." It's an unusual phrase, but what a great picture! It says our burden is too heavy for us to lift; it must be rolled. So when we are anxious, we roll those burdens over for Him to carry.

Yet that also presumes something very, very important: our plans must be *able* to be rolled to begin with. Whatever we want to build, it must be God's right design from the beginning. Rather than, "OK, God, here's what I want to do. I am building this blocky square-shaped thing, and committing it to you" we must say, "Lord, what are *your* designs for me, that I might follow you? Are you leading me to this business or this dating app? Or do you want to provide for me another way?"

Proverbs 16:3 doesn't mean we pray for what we want, and it will happen. As far as we are able, we should try to do what is in keeping with *His* plan for us, then roll our burdens over to Him.

Reflection

How do you respond to the call to roll your burden to Jesus for Him to carry? Is there something in your life that you might not *want* to roll over to God? Something you want to design your own way? If so, confess it to the Lord and ask Him to show you where *He* is leading you.

"You never know where God wants to take you unless you allow Him to actually lead."

—Krista Skytland

Day 52

My Father's house has many rooms; if that were not so,
would I have told you that I am going there to prepare a place for you?

—John 14:2

We Will Never Be Truly Comfortable Here

A particular national park had once been a beautiful destination, with nature trails and a large clearing overlooking breathtaking views. But when budget cuts led to a lack of oversight, that clearing attracted long-term campers. And with no bathrooms or bulk trash disposal, it was soon so overwhelmed with trash and waste that visitors stopped coming and even the squatters found it distasteful.

The park simply wasn't equipped to be a place to live. Trying to make a beautiful stopping place into a residence led to difficulty and discomfort, which reminded the residents that it wasn't built as a permanent home.

We need to be reminded of that same thing about our world—and God often uses difficulties and discomfort to do it.

It is so easy to lose hope when we see sickness, aging, war, loneliness, constant toil, and so many other heartaches. We forget that all these troubles come because we are living in a world corrupted by sin, one that can never be our true home.

Even worse, like the futile effort of trying to find solace by living in a park, we tend to actively seek comfort and hope in the things of this fallen world instead of those of the world to come. We get intense about going to the gym to try to look better and feel better about ourselves. We seek affirmation from a relationship, from being a good mom, or from being lauded as the company's best store manager in the whole state.

We are hoping to finally feel comfortable, *but God doesn't want us to find comfort in those things*! So we feel discontent instead.

Through our discomfort, God allows us to be constantly reminded that these places where we are looking for contentment are not built for that purpose. There's nothing wrong with wanting to be healthy and fit. Or working to be a great store manager. But God has set it up so that those earthly things will never give us true happiness.

God wants fellowship with Him to be the only basis for our satisfaction. He wants our hearts to yearn for that—to yearn for heaven, not for the things of this world. So when we feel discouraged or lonely, let's use that prompt to remember that this world is just a stopping place, and that there is another Place, overlooking a far more beautiful vista, that is in fact built to be our home.

Reflection

What difficulty has left you feeling discouraged or disappointed? How can it be traced back to the brokenness of this world? Does remembering that this world is not our permanent home "reframe" that difficulty and give you hope? How can you build the habit of remembering that truth?

"Our Father refreshes us on the journey with some pleasant inns, but will not encourage us to mistake them for home."

—C. S. Lewis

Day 53

Therefore, having put away falsehood, let each one of you speak the truth with his neighbor, for we are members one of another.

—**Ephesians 4:25,** ESV

The Salt of Truth

Some time ago, I received an email from a friend. A well-known organization was about to launch an initiative that would damage many people and our culture. My friend urgently asked me and several others to pass this information along so that many people could contact the organization and brainstorm other ways to right this terrible wrong.

I forwarded the email to a few people, but something didn't sound quite right. So I sought more information and discovered that the accusations were untrue. This organization was not even considering such an initiative. The leaders did not hold the beliefs being attributed to them, and explained that they, too, would be concerned if the rumors were true! I found myself greatly respecting the grace with which the leaders handled the challenge.

I sent some of what I learned to my rallying friends, saying, "This doesn't appear to be accurate, and if we've already passed it along to anyone [which all of us had] we should probably go back and tell those people we were wrong."

In today's culture of misinformation and distrust, you've undoubtedly experienced similar situations. But here's the thing: this story was from more than twenty years ago. Misinformation is nothing new, in part because it is a favorite strategy of the enemy. Remember the Garden? The enemy knows how to twist a lie *juuuust enough* to make it sound like truth. It becomes easy for us to believe something that seems so convincing.

Yet Jesus calls us to be salt and light to a decaying and dark world, and He calls us to share truth. Which is one reason He also commands us to be very careful with our communications. If something sounds "off," we must hold it up to the light to confirm whether it is true. If accusations are made against a brother or sister in Christ, we must ask God how to handle it with grace. If something "needs sharing," we must choose to share in a redemptive way—or maybe not at all. Because when we share messages laced with untruth, gossip, or condemnation, we unwittingly spread toxins instead of salt and light. Toxins infect, grow, and ultimately kill, while salt seasons, preserves, heals, and disinfects.

Wherever hope lives, truth and love form its foundation. Let us season every conversation, every relationship, every circumstance with both.

Reflection

Have there been times you shared something you later realized was wrong? Or shared something that might have been true but perhaps shouldn't have been shared? Write a prayer for God to grant you discernment and wisdom in today's culture.

"He that takes truth for his guide and duty for his end may safely trust to God's providence to lead him aright."

—Blaise Pascal

Day 54

But those who drink the water I
give will never be thirsty again.
It becomes a fresh, bubbling spring
within them, giving them eternal life.

—John 4:14, NLT

Hope Makes Us Brave

It was odd for a woman to draw water at noon, alone. The other women had come hours ago, drawing water as they chattered away, enjoying the coolness of the morning. But not this woman. She was thirsty—and not just for water. She was probably feeling rejected by her community and taking the easy way out; avoiding the eye rolls by avoiding people.

But today a Jewish teacher was sitting at the well. He asked her for a drink. Startled that He would drink from the cup of a woman—let alone a Samaritan!—her curiosity was sparked. He advised her to ask Him for living water, promising springs that would slake her thirst forever.

Hope whispered life to her long-withered heart. "I know that Messiah is coming" (John 4:25). Quietly He released the news—the first person recorded in Scripture to receive it—"I am he" (John 4:26).

Hope gushed like a geyser. And what came from it? Courage! Bonds of shame and fear fell away as she raced to town, rushing to share the news with those who had rejected her. "Come, see a man who told me everything I ever did. Could this be the Messiah?" (John 4:29).

Her fellow Samaritans, suddenly aware of their own thirst, believed. Some believed her on the spot, sight unseen, and trusted Jesus for the brimming promise of eternal life. Others, compelled by her testimony, rushed to the well to hear Him. Then they too believed. What a beautiful cycle! The woman was filled with hope, which gave her the courage to share Jesus with others, which fueled her hope even more.

Do you want to be more courageous in sharing about Jesus? Are there other actions you know you should take but you've been avoiding? Maybe you're supposed to reconcile with someone, but you quail at the idea of reaching out. Maybe you feel God wants you to apply for a *huge* promotion but are worried about being embarrassed. Maybe you're being nudged to share God's love with a relative whom you feel has always judged you.

Friends, in this journey together, we've been seeing how casting out fear and building hope creates a positive cycle. As we draw on Jesus' wellspring of life, it begins a beautiful cycle of courage as we share that life with others.

Reflection

Is there an area of your life in which you are thirsty for more than water? Or an area in which you are afraid to take action? Thank God for giving you Living Water through Jesus, and ask for His guidance on one step of courage He would have you take. Journal what happens.

"My witness and impact is directly proportional to my willingness to regularly count the cost."

—Eric Ryan

Day 55

He who did not spare His own Son, but delivered Him over for us all, how will He not also with Him freely give us all things?

—**Romans 8:32**, NASB

Infinite Mercy

Have you ever noticed that although God miraculously rescues the Israelites from the Egyptians, supernaturally guides them, and feeds them in the wilderness, they immediately doubt His goodness each time new fears crop up? "Have you brought us up from Egypt to kill us?" they ask Moses when they reach a location where no water is visible (Exodus 17:3, NASB). Because they cannot see how their needs will be met, they assume God has bad intentions toward them.

We are more like the Israelites than we care to admit, especially when we are afraid. We trust God when things are going well ("Thank You, Lord, for this new job!"), but when circumstances begin to look shaky, we may begin to doubt His goodness. ("Lord, did you bring me to this job just to drop a bomb on me? It isn't working out! At least in the old job I had health insurance!")

We would almost certainly get frustrated with a friend who doubted and complained about us the way the Israelites constantly doubted and complained about God. I'm so thankful God is not like us! (<sigh of relief>) So thankful that God's supply of mercy is so great, there is nothing we can do to deplete it. We give so little thanks for His blessings and do so much grumbling about the challenges—yet far from giving us the punishment we deserve, God's reaction to our sin is to allow His beloved Son to take on that punishment so *we* won't receive it!

Here's why this matters: *If we were to truly understand God's infinite mercy, we would never lack hope.* If He loves us enough to make the ultimate sacrifice, even though we *so* don't deserve it, why would we *not* assume He has our ultimate best in mind?

After all, God didn't abandon the Israelites when they did that complaining-about-no-water thing; He brought water from a rock. God never leaves us to fend for ourselves, no matter how great the provocation. Through Christ, we complainers are saved from God's wrath and promised eternal life. And here on earth, we are promised that in God's omnipotence, He will ensure that even these things that we worry and complain about will somehow work together for our ultimate good (Romans 8:28). That is a promise that only God can keep. And He always does. So the next time you need hope, look no further than our God's infinite, undeserved mercy.

Reflection

In what ways have you learned to
trust more and complain against God
less since you started this devotional?

"We have this for a foundation truth, that there is more mercy in Christ than sin in us."

—Richard Sibbes

Day 56

Martha said to Jesus, "Lord, if only you had been here, my brother would not have died. But even now I know that God will give you whatever you ask."

—John 11:21-22, NLT

"But Even Now . . ."

Lazarus was dead. It was the end of his story. And Mary and Martha, his sisters, were now without a provider or protector. They were devastated and vulnerable. Their hope seemed lost.

Are you in the middle of a Lazarus moment and experiencing loss of hope in some way? Has your source of provision or security seemingly passed out of reach? Perhaps a dream has gone unfulfilled, and you're grieving.

As we read the Lazarus story in John 11, we find a model for moments when we must accept something hard that has happened, something we think couldn't possibly be part of a loving God's plan. Because acceptance happens one of two ways: with or without hope.

Acceptance without hope leads to despair. And when you believe there is no loving God on the other side of a hard outcome, despair makes logical sense.

Yet this story models another type of acceptance.

Think about how you and I would feel in Mary and Martha's shoes. After all, Jesus was a dear friend. They had seen His direct line to the Father and watched Him work miracle after miracle. If you or I had a tragedy looming, and our friend Jesus delayed and seemingly refused to come in our time of greatest need, I suspect we would not only be heartbroken—we would feel deeply angry and betrayed. And when Jesus arrived, the sisters did indeed have very human reactions: Why had He not come sooner?!

But now comes Martha's example to us for whenever we think Jesus is refusing to help in our time of need. She tells Him, "But even now I know that God will give you whatever you ask of Him." Her response says, "Even when all looks lost, *God is able*."

The same woman who earlier struggled with petty grievances (Luke 10:40-42) now has acceptance *with hope*. She accepts Jesus' sovereignty and decision to allow Lazarus to die . . . and she also states her trust in Him. Her hope isn't found in the outcome she longs for, but in knowing that Jesus is in control no matter what.

This is next-level trust. And in this journey together, this is where God has been leading each of us. Even when logic would say all hope is lost, we *still* have hope. That's because with God, a particular outcome may be hard, but it is *never* the true end of the story.

Reflection

Martha's faith clearly grew over time: from her jealousy that Mary wasn't helping serve guests (Luke 10:38-42) to having both acceptance and great faith that Jesus could heal her brother. What might have led to that shift? And what actions might lead to such a shift in your heart as well? (For example, joining a discipleship small group or journaling daily about God's goodness.)

"An evidence that our will has been broken is that we begin to thank God for that which once seemed so bitter, knowing that His will is good and that, in His time and in His way, He is able to make the most bitter waters sweet."

–Nancy DeMoss Wolgemuth

Day 57

Teach those who are rich in this world not to be proud and not to trust in their money, which is so unreliable. Their trust should be in God . . . always being ready to share with others. By doing this they will be storing up their treasure as a good foundation for the future so that they may experience true life.

—1 Timothy 6:17-19, NLT

Plan for the Right Future

A few years ago, Jeff and I researched and wrote a book called *Thriving in Love & Money*. Money is one of the big issues in marriage, so we weren't trying to help couples *manage* money well but to help them have a great *relationship* around money.

What hit me was how unusual that approach was. Millions of people spend a ton of time and energy thinking about financial planning—saving money, getting out of debt, looking for good returns, and preparing for retirement. But we aren't as attuned to thinking about and planning for the non-financial aspects of money: how to build a great marriage around money, how to trust God through tithing, how to use our financial resources for the Kingdom of God and store up treasures in heaven (Matthew 6:20).

Friends, I think we have it backwards, and that creates struggles with hope. It is fine to have hopes and plans for the future. But we have to be sure to hope and plan for the *right* future!

Life doesn't end with passing on any remaining assets to our kids. If we know Jesus, our eternal souls simply move from an earthly home to a heavenly home. Ann Lamott says, "We Christians like to think of death as a major change of address." We pass through this life and on to the next, where we will either have treasures stored up . . . or not.

God asks us to use our resources—energy, time, money—for Kingdom purposes. And we "should be rich in good works and generous to those in need" (1 Timothy 6:18, NLT). This goes beyond tithing and giving. Eternity will be filled with souls whom we can invest in right now. We should put at least as much energy into figuring out how to bring dinner to an exhausted single mom as we do into figuring out how to cheaply buy tech stocks. We should put at least as much effort into making our home the place neighborhood kids hang out, and investing in their lives, as we do into renovating and increasing its resale value.

This doesn't mean ignoring our earthly future; the Bible exhorts us to be financially prudent as well. But all our resources ultimately exist for *God's* purposes, not just ours. Let's always keep that in mind and store up treasures for eternity. Let's hope and plan for the right future.

Reflection

List some ways you are storing up for your earthly future and some ways you are storing up treasures in heaven. How can you plan to do more of the latter?

"Giving is not God's way of raising money. It's God's way of raising people into the likeness of His Son."

—Author Unknown

Day 58

Be still, and know that I am God.

—Psalm 46:10

Be Still and Hope

Have you ever seen so much evidence of something negative in your future that you're afraid to hope? Your child has gone a long way down a damaging road. Your spouse has hired a divorce lawyer. You're being evicted. Will things ever change? Instead of pressing forward in an attitude of prayer and trust, misguided self-preservation pushes you to shut down and protect your heart from disappointment.

You're not alone. In 2 Kings 18 and 19 we see the bloodthirsty Assyrian army besieging King Hezekiah and God's people. Surrounding Jerusalem, they taunt the Israelites and their God. The people tremble with fear. Vastly outnumbered, death or surrender seem inevitable. Their hopeless hearts crumble.

Not so for King Hezekiah. He girded himself for battle of a different sort. He went straight into the Temple of God, where he prayed with the heart of a warrior: "Now, LORD our God, deliver us . . . so that all the kingdoms of the earth may know that you alone, LORD, are God" (2 Kings 19:19). That very night, the Angel of the Lord descended and put to death 185,000 Assyrian soldiers. Biblical scholars suggest that Psalm 46 might have been written as a direct response to this deliverance and victory: "Come, see the glorious works of the LORD. . . . 'Be still, and know that I am God! I will be honored by every nation.' . . . The LORD of Heaven's Armies is here among us" (Psalm 46:8, 10-11, NLT).

Friends, *the God who rescued His people then is still our God today.* If you have lost hope, if the enemy is warring at the gates of your life and you see no way out, God may be asking you to go into the temple and cry out to Him to save you. Not just to save you from the circumstances, but to save you from your hopelessness, your fear, your loneliness, the weight of your sin. And then to simply be still. To realize that your deliverance is in His hands, not yours. To wait, watch, and pray with active expectation, knowing that *He is GOD,* the creator of the universe.

Today, let yourself rest in God's power that shows up best when we are hopeless and helpless to act in our own defense. The hope God offers doesn't depend on what we can see, but on the God who is glorious in battle on our behalf, who commands all the angels of heaven. Be still and let Him fight for you today.

Reflection

In what area of your life do you have the most difficult time remaining hopeful? When faced with uncertainty, what keeps you from placing your hope in the Lord? What would you do differently today, if you were to "be still and know" that He is God? Give it a try.

"Darkness comes. In the middle of it, the future looks blank. The temptation to quit is huge. Don't. You are in good company . . . You will argue with yourself that there is no way forward. But with God, nothing is impossible. He has more ropes and ladders and tunnels out of pits than you can conceive. Wait. Pray without ceasing. Hope."

–John Piper

Day 59

"Whoever pursues righteousness and love finds life, prosperity and honor."

—Proverbs 21:21

The Gifts of a Transparent Life

Not long ago, a friend became the CEO of a business with many locations. He was hired by a parent company to "clean up" the chaotic and unprofitable operations. Thankfully, he was a leader of integrity who could both make the tough decisions ("sadly, this location needs to be closed") and be a caring manager. Most employees loved him and were relieved things were turning around.

One employee who wasn't was a longtime executive who was placed under review for poor performance. This executive tried to undercut the new CEO and stir up trouble. He would have to go.

The day he planned to terminate this executive, our friend was summoned into a meeting with the parent company. A serious harassment claim had just been made against him. It was obvious who was behind it.

There was no evidence to the charge. But in the cultural climate, the corporation felt compelled to launch a wide-ranging investigation. Even though they found nothing, our friend was fired.

When we face injustice, the last thing we might describe feeling is "peace" or "a sense of hope." But I was struck by how our friend had *both.* He leads a discipleship group for teen boys, and he told them, "We've talked about the importance of being an open book, right? That's why I was at peace during the investigation. I knew that if I lost my job, it would be because of false accusations, not because of hiding something that might be found out. And now I trust God to bring another answer."

Living a transparent life is a powerful engine for peace, hope, joy, and other characteristics we long for. Proverbs 21 says if we pursue righteousness, we get other beautiful things thrown in: life, prosperity, and honor. But a life of integrity does not happen naturally. It means making good daily choices as we walk onward in our journey to hope. It means being an open book at the office. It means we don't hide anything from our spouse—they can see all our text messages, money, passwords, and frivolous online purchases. It means we live in purity and trust God to care for us.

Our friend was soon hired by another company to run their whole network because of his reputation for integrity. His choice to pursue righteousness led him to prosperity and honor, just as God promised him—and just as God promises us.

Reflection

Who is someone in your life who lives a transparent life and has qualities you admire? How might you emulate them? What are some ways you don't always live transparently? Write down three things you want to do differently and commit before God to doing them.

"What is meant by a 'pure heart' is this: one that is watching and pondering what God says and replacing its own ideas with the Word of God."

—Martin Luther

Day 60

Now faith is confidence in what we hope for and assurance about what we do not see.

—Hebrews 11:1

Looking Back, Moving Forward

We have been on a learning journey toward Hope with a capital "H." As we step forward into the next phase of living it out every day, let me ask you a question:

What have you seen God do to increase your hope in Him during this time? In a moment, you'll have the chance to write down that answer. And I pray it will actually take a bit of time because you've had your eyes opened to so *many* ways God has worked in your life!

Remembering what God has done for us in the past is one of the most crucial elements of finding hope for the future. It is the reason God had the Israelites pile up stones from the Jordan River after He provided a miraculous crossing into the Promised Land (Joshua 4). It's a key reason God told His children to celebrate several different festivals honoring God's goodness (such as the Feast of Tabernacles). And it is why Jesus broke the bread, looked down through history at all of us, and said, "Do this in remembrance of Me."

Our God knew that His children would face giants as they worked to take the Land of Promise. They would need reminding that their all-powerful God was with them. He knew they would face seasons of uncertainty, rebellion, and occupation and would need regular reminders of His provision and the coming Messiah. He knew they would get caught up in the turmoil of life or the weight of sin and need to be brought back to the cross.

We need those reminders too. They build our faith—our *confident* faith—even when things are hard.

Let's remember all the way back to the opening note of this devotional book. As we said, in the midst of worry (about school, marriage, finances, etc.) God wants us to have a true sense of hope even when we don't see specific evidence that things are "looking up," right?

Well, when we look back in remembrance we will, quite often, have the perspective to see just how many times that has happened . . . and just how true this statement has been in our lives:

[W]e know that suffering produces perseverance; perseverance, character; and character, hope. And hope does not put us to shame, because God's love has been poured out into our hearts through the Holy Spirit, who has been given to us.

—Romans 5:3-5

When we look back at what God has done in our lives, we can see how He used times of worry and suffering to produce perseverance and character in us. With the benefit of distance, we often *do* see the evidence of how He was working even when we didn't see it at the time.

The end result is hope. Those things were hard, but God was creating in us a hope that can't be created or faked or built on anything other than Him.

Suddenly, Hebrews 11:1 feels so real, even in the next time of worry. Faith is indeed the confidence in what we hope for! We are assured about what we do not yet see. Most importantly, we know that our heavenly Father is there. That He is working. And that He loves us with an everlasting love.

Friends, we can forever hope in that.

Reflection

Go back through the devotional and read what you wrote in response to the Reflection sections. Circle anything particularly important that God showed you.

Pick three of the most important insights that God gave you over these 60 days, and write them here. How can you remember those to give you strength for the future?

What have you seen God do to increase your hope in Him during this time? (For example, perhaps He has been very faithful in an area of need.) Take some time thinking about this, and jot down everything you can remember. Come back to this page in the coming days if you think of other things.

What one thing do you feel God would have you do differently as a result of this journey to hope? Write that commitment here to the Lord.

"Go in peace
to love and serve
the Lord."

—Pastoral blessing

With My Thanks...

This devotional has been a labor of love by many people. I wish there was a way to adequately thank everyone who contributed, but I have to at least share my love and gratitude for a core group.

First, to the original iDisciple / Family Christian crew, thank you for leading the way in equipping believers to follow Jesus. To David Henriksen, Kobus Johnsen, John Crowe, Q Robinson, and Carlisa Flournoy: our whole team appreciates you so much. We have been praying for God to bless each of you as you move into your next adventure. To Annabelle Grobler, we especially appreciate your beautiful designs: we find hope just by looking at them! And to our amazing editor, Nancy Taylor, thank you for turning my long-winded messages into something that immediately ushers women into the presence of God.

I'm very, very grateful for the team of women writers who brought their passion, wisdom, and talent to bear on this project, including Beth Peazzoni, Heather Van Wyck, Sue Birdseye, Christina Williams, Heather Hargis, Kelsey Privett, Kim Patton, Kristi Wagner, Sarah Geringer, and Manda Hart. Thank you, *thank you,* ladies, for listening to so many of my rambling audio recordings and turning each one into a special and readable draft! Special thanks to Cami Summers for your insightful suggestions on many Reflection sections, and to my mom, Judy Reidinger, for her proofreading prowess. And extra-special thanks to Cindy Fahy for listening to God and offering your help, especially in the middle of your own time of looking toward the hope of heaven for your father.

I'm particularly grateful for my core team, especially my amazing staff director Eileen Kirkland, who runs the whole ministry one day and edits devotionals the next, and Amy Masaschi, my executive assistant who brought her own wisdom to this devotional while also ensuring I showed up at the right hotel for the right speaking engagement in the midst of all the writing! Thanks to Laura Warner for holding up Charlyn's arms on this project, as well as to Samantha Griggs, Nicole Owens, Kristy Floyd, and Suzanne Stewman for keeping things running—and for always sharing hope while half of the team was exhausted and trying to find it! And to Charlyn Elliott, staff director Emeritus and Grand Task Master for this devotional: there are no words that can adequately express my gratitude for you. I'm inspired not only by your skill but by your faithfulness to God's callings. Thank you.

To my longtime senior editor and friend, Katie Phillips . . . what will I do without you? Your heart for this ministry, your skill as a writer, your passion for reaching women through these devotionals, your wisdom, and your steadfast counsel and support have been so precious to me ever since our big strong college guys were little dudes on the playground. I *promise* I'm not bitter about our publisher stealing you away for a full-time job. (David, I *promise* that if someone teepees your house it was someone else.) But I also promise that you're stuck with me as a friend for life.

To my precious family, Jeff, Morgen, and Luke: thanks for always showing me love, doing everything around the house when I'm on a book deadline, praying for me, encouraging me when I'm downcast . . . and helping me Find Hope.

Finally, to the Author of all: All of us are humbled and speechless at the immensity of Your love and the privilege of being used for Your Kingdom. May these words be anointed by You.

Sources

DAY 1 — R.C. Sproul, "Right Now Counts Forever," *Tabletalk Magazine* (May 1977).

DAY 2 — Charles Spurgeon, AZQuotes.com, https://www.azquotes.com/quote/446641.

DAY 3 — Albert Einstein Quotes, BrainyQuote.com, https://www.brainyquote.com/quotes/albert_einstein_390808.

DAY 4 — Francois Fenelon, AZQuotes.com, https://www.azquotes.com/quote/547638.

DAY 5 — Karle Wilson Baker, "Courage," *Poetry Magazine* (October 1921): 16.

DAY 6 — John Piper, "God Is Always Doing 10,000 Things in Your Life," *Desiring God* (blog), January 1, 2013, https://www.desiringgod.org /articles/god-is-always-doing-10000-things-in-your-life.

DAY 7 — Bob Goff, Twitter, November 22, 2014, 2019, https://twitter.com/bobgoff/status/536170317018697728.

DAY 8 — Heraclitus, Goodreads.com, https://www.goodreads.com/quotes/645349-the-content-of-your-character-is-your-choice-day-by.

DAY 9 — Nightbirde, "God is on the Bathroom Floor," *Nightbirde* (blog), March 9, 2021, https://www.nightbirde.co/blog/2021/9/27/god-is-on-the-bathroom-floor.

DAY 10 — Andy Stanley, Irresistible: *Reclaiming the New That Jesus Unleashed for the World* (Grand Rapids, MI: Zondervan, 2018), 216.

DAY 11 — Max Lucado, *Traveling Light: Releasing the Burdens You Were Never Meant to Bear* (Nashville, TN: Thomas Nelson, 2013), 77.

DAY 12 — Aiden Wilson Tozer, *The Pursuit of God Updated, Annotated* (Aneko Press: Kindle Edition), 61.

DAY 13 — Jackie Hill Perry, *Holier Than Thou: How God's Holiness Help Us Trust Him* (Nashville, TN: B&H Publishing, 2021), 2.

DAY 14 — David Steindl-Rast, *Gratefulness: The Heart of Prayer: An Approach to Life in Full* (Mahwah, NJ: Paulist Press, 1984), 204

DAY 15 — C. S. Lewis, *Mere Christianity (C.S. Lewis Signature Classics,* HarperCollins ebooks: Kindle Edition, 2009), 136–137.

DAY 16 — Beth Moore, *Breaking Free: Discover the Victory of Total Surrender* (Nashville, TN: B & H Books, 2007), 157.

DAY 17 — Oswald Chambers, *The Highest Good with The Pilgrim's Song Book and Thy Great Redemption* (Kindle Edition: Discovery House, 2015), 613.

DAY 18 — Priscilla Shirer, AZQuotes, https://www.azquotes.com/quote/822983.

DAY 19 — Amelia Earhart, "Quotes," AmeliaEarhart.com, https://ameliaearhart.com/quotes/.

DAY 20 — "Gratitude in the Suffering," *Mercy Multiplied* (blog), November 28, 2016, https://mercymultiplied.com/gratitude-in-the-suffering/.

DAY 21 — Mo Huggins, sermon, July 10 ,2022 (Mountain West Church, Stone Mountain GA); used by permission.

DAY 22 — Gary Thomas, *When to Walk Away: Finding Freedom From Toxic People* (Grand Rapids, MI: Zondervan, 2019), 16.

DAY 23 — Rick Warren, "Worry About Nothing; Pray About Everything—Daily Hope with Rick Warren," Crosswalk.com, June 28, 2022, https://www.crosswalk.com/devotionals/daily-hope-with-rick-warren/daily-hope-with-rick-warren-june-28-2022.html.

DAY 24 — Hudson Taylor, AZQuotes.com, https://www.azquotes.com/quote/392763.

DAY 25 — C. S. Lewis, *Mere Christianity* (C. S. Lewis Signature Classics, Kindle Edition: HarperCollins ebooks, 2009), 176.

DAY 26 — AZQuotes.com, https://www.azquotes.com/quote/645274; *quote is attributed to W.C.Fields. It is also sometimes attributed to Dorothy Parker, therefore it is listed as Author Unknown.

DAY 27 — Priscilla Shirer, *Fervent: A Woman's Battle Plan to Serious, Specific and Strategic Prayer* (Nashville, TN: B & H Publishing, 2015), 5.

DAY 28 — Crawford Loritts, *Unshaken: Real Faith in Our Faithful God* (Wheaton, IL: Crossway, 2015).

DAY 29 — John Donne, *Devotions Upon Emergent Occasions Together with Death's Duel* (Kindle Edition: A Public Domain book), 63.

DAY 30 — C. Joybell C., MoreFamousQuotes.com, https://www.morefamousquotes.com/authors/c-joybell-c-quotes/.

DAY 31 — Minnie Lou Haskins, *Desert: God Knows (The Gate of the Year)* as quoted by King George VI, Christmas Broadcast, December 25, 1939.

DAY 32 — Maya Angelou, Maya Angelou Author Page, April 17, 2022, https://www.facebook.com/MayaAngelou/posts/10161014554754796.

DAY 33 — Billy Graham, Twitter, April 26, 2020, https://twitter.com/billygraham/status/1254505533404598278.

DAY 34 — African Proverbs Quotes, Allauthor.com, https://allauthor.com/quotes/166383/.

DAY 35 — Joyce Brothers, AZ Quotes.com, https://www.azquotes.com/quote/37496.

DAY 36 — George Eliot, *Middlemarch* (Kindle Edition: Duke Classics, 2012; first published 1874), 1297.

DAY 37 — Larry Crabb, AZQuotes.com, https://www.azquotes.com/quote/1521845.

DAY 38 — Timothy Keller, *Walking with God through Pain and Suffering* (London: Penguin Books, 2015), 180-181.

DAY 39 — Author Unknown, Daystar Television Network, Facebook post, January 24, 2015, Facebook.com, https://www.facebook.com/DaystarTV/

DAY 40 — Corrie ten Boom, AZQuotes.com, https://www.azquotes.com/quote/1390191.

DAY 41 — Father Sean Magaldi, "Are You Afraid to Talk to Jesus?", *St. Patrick's Roman Catholic Church,* Smithtown, NY (From the Pastor's Desk blog), August 5, 2018, https://www.stpatricksmithtown.org/

DAY 42 — Max Lucado, *Every Day Deserves a Chance: Wake Up to the Gift of 24 Hours* (Nashville TN: Thomas Nelson, Inc., 2007), 142.

DAY 43 — Mark Hall, Casting Crowns Concert, First Baptist Church, Woodstock GA, October 28, 2022.

DAY 44 — Miles McPherson, AZQuotes.com, https ://www.azquotes.com/quote/913044.

DAY 45 — R. C. Sproul, Jr., QuoteFancy.com, https://quotefancy.com/quote/1676458.

DAY 46 — Andrew Peterson, Behold the Lamb of God Concert, Perimeter Church, Johns Creek GA, December 2, 2021.

DAY 47 — Arthur C. Brooks, "No One Cares!", *The Atlantic*, November 11, 2021, https://www.theatlantic.com/family/archive/2021/11/how-stop-caring-what-other-people-think-you/620670/

DAY 48 — Henri Nouwen, *Bread for the Journey: A Daybook of Wisdom and Faith* (New York: Harper Collins, 2009),29.

DAY 49 — Lysa TerKeurst, *Uninvited: Living Loved When You Feel Less Than, Left-Out and Lonely* (Nashville, TN: Thomas Nelson, 2016), 23.

DAY 50 — Author Unknown (Note: This quote is often incorrectly attributed to Charles Spurgeon, as noted by The Spurgeon Center. https://www.spurgeon.org/resource-library/blog-entries/6-quotes-spurgeon-didnt-say/.)

DAY 51 — Krista Skytland, *The Marriage Collective*, Winshape Retreat Center, Rome GA, October 28, 2022.

DAY 52 — C. S.Lewis, *The Problem of Pain* (New York: Harper Collins, 1940), 117

DAY 53 — Blaise Pascal, BrainyQuote.com, https://www.brainyquote.com/quotes/blaise_pascal_388828.

DAY 54 — Eric Ryan, sermon, June 12 2021 (Perimeter Church, Johns Creek, GA).

DAY 55 — Richard Sibbes, *The Bruised Reed* (Carlisle, PA: Banner of Truth Trust, revised edition 2021), 13.

DAY 56 — Nancy Leigh DeMoss, *A Place of Quiet Rest: Finding Intimacy with God Through a Daily Devotional Life* (Chicago, IL: Moody, 2000), 70.

DAY 57 — Anne Lamott, *12 Truths I Learned from Life and Writing"* (TED Talk, 2017), https://www.ted.com/talks/anne_lamott_12_truths_i_learned_from_life_and_writing.

DAY 58 — John Piper, "John Piper Quotes," BrainyQuote.com. https://www.brainyquote.com/quotes/john_piper_605818.

DAY 59 — Martin Luther, *Luther's Works*, vol. 21: *The Sermon on the Mount and the Magnificat*, ed. J. J. Pelikan, H. C. Oswald, & H. T. Lehmann (Saint Louis: Concordia Publishing House).

DAY 60 — Pastoral blessing